Contents

Speaking Up

Millicent Fenwick

Speaking Up

Foreword by Norman Cousins

HARPER & ROW, PUBLISHERS, New York
Cambridge, Philadelphia, San Francisco, London
Mexico City, São Paulo, Sydney   *1817*

We would like to thank the Oral History Research Office of Columbia University for their cooperation.

Portions of this work first appeared in *The Philadelphia Bulletin* and *Newsday*.

"Special Interest and Special Privilege" first appeared in the *Washington Post*, August 24, 1976, under the title "Congressional Reform—A View from the Inside."

"Advice to the Secretary of State" first appeared in the Summer 1980 issue of *Foreign Policy* magazine, #39, under the title "Speaking Frankly."

"A Question of Honor" first appeared in the February 23, 1976 issue of *The New York Times*. Copyright © 1976 by The New York Times Company. Reprinted by permission.

"Initiation in Foreign Affairs" first appeared in the March 21, 1975 issue of *The New York Times* under the title "Military Aid for Vietnam and Cambodia? No." Copyright © 1975 by The New York Times Company. Reprinted by permission.

"The 'Royalty Complex' " first appeared in the October 5, 1978 issue of the *Christian Science Monitor* under the title "Congress Must Give Up Its Royalty Complex." Reprinted by permission.

Publisher's Note: All of the author's proceeds from this book are donated to selected educational institutions in the state of New Jersey.

FIRST EDITION

Designed by Ruth Bornschlegel

Library of Congress Cataloging in Publication Data

Fenwick, Millicent.
  Speaking up.

  1. United States—Politics and government—1981–   .
  2. United States—Politics and government—1977–1981.
  3. Fenwick, Millicent.   I. Title.
E876.F46   1982   320.973   81-48238
ISBN 0-06-015003-3   AACR2

82 83 84 85 86 10 9 8 7 6 5 4 3 2 1

*To the people of the
Fifth Congressional District
who sent me to Washington
as their representative.*

Foreword

Having been born and having spent my early years in New Jersey—several of them not far from Bernardsville, where Millicent Fenwick makes her home—I feel the tug of a special connection to the state. Robert Burns said it for everyone who is nourished by youthful ties when he wrote that his heart was always in the highlands where he was born. When good things happen to New Jersey, I like to dwell on them. And one of the best things that has happened to New Jersey in recent years is Millicent Fenwick. She represents that combination of intelligence, fairness, openness, good will, and good humor that has won her high respect in the Congress and among those who have followed her work.

The Watergate affair was an American ordeal. It was also a regenerating experience. If it produced disillusion about specific personalities, it also produced a new and higher regard for American institutions in general and for the Congress in particular. The general tendency to take members of Congress lightly was as much a casualty of Watergate hearings as was the credibilty of the chief targets of the investigation. Anyone who followed the television hearings of the House Judiciary Committee was impressed with the quality of its members. Instead of the stereotyped picture of the Congressman as a pork-barreling, tunnel-visioned officeholder, there emerged a new image of the responsible, serious-minded, and well-informed public servant. It is a picture that would have been deeply reassuring to historical observers like de Tocqueville and Edmund Burke, who naturally wondered whether the highest deliberative body in the nation would attract deliberate men. Few developments in twentieth-century America have been more encouraging than the change in the public attitude toward Congress as the result of the full view of its representatives made possible by the televised hearings.

Millicent Fenwick was not involved in those hearings but her special qualities do full justice to the enlarged expectations that many Americans today hold of the people they elect to Congress. The newsletters she writes to her constituents are a model of sober reflection and effective presentation. They reflect a zest for public service. Her discussion of important issues in these letters is anything but doctrinaire or defensive. It becomes quickly apparent that her main purpose in these letters is not to justify her voting positions but to share with her fellow citizens the results of her pursuit of principle on vital questions. Her analysis of the facts is open and honest. In this sense, her letters and papers constitute a knowledgeable guided tour of the main issues before the American people. Her political affiliation is secondary to her independence of mind and spirit.

Heroic figures in the American past, like Justice Oliver Wendell Holmes and Judge Learned Hand, would have welcomed her as a legislator of generous spirit and penetrating intelligence who could be counted upon to use her abundant good sense and good will in advancing the general welfare. She has a keen sense of American history and a profound respect for the young thinkers who two hundred years ago came together in Philadelphia to do something that had never before been done in quite that way or on quite that scale; namely, to design a structure and political system based on the lessons of history and the enlightened aspirations of thinking people. She is living proof that public servants can be effective and responsible without being tagged as primarily conservative or liberal. She is liberal in the sense that she is deeply responsive to human needs; she is conservative in the sense that she is distrustful of power. She believes that government has the obligation to attend to the general welfare but she also knows how important it is to guard the American people against those in authority who would expand their power at the expense of the public interest. So she picks her way carefully, striking a balance between support of those things that only government can do, and opposition to any action or trend in government that weakens the principle that the ultimate power must rest in the hands of the people.

For example, she is not easily gulled by calls for higher military spending that she rightly regards as an end in itself. She sees no security for the American people in military budgets that foster vast waste and overlap. She recognizes the danger to American institutions from the arms race. She sees the direct connection between the need for world institutions that can deal with basic causes of war and the creation of genuine security for America or anyone else.

Millicent Fenwick is a thinking person who believes in the importance of ideas and who seeks to relate the national interest to the human interest. Her book is as much a tribute to the people who make it possible for her to serve the American community as a whole as it is to her own independence of mind and action.

—NORMAN COUSINS

Preface

This is mostly a book of letters to the people of the Fifth District of New Jersey who sent me down to Congress in the elections of 1974. Interspersed are articles and "letters to the Editor" from various newspapers, transcripts of interviews, and excerpts from debates on the floor of the House. It is a mixed bag—disjointed as such a gathering-together of thoughts must surely be. But I hope it does express some of the flavor and vitality of our congressional system. I hope it honestly portrays the way things really are, and some of the issues that faced us in these years.

To me, it is a never-ending wonder that I am here at all. When I see the Capitol dome at the end of the street, lighted against the dark, early-morning sky, I am still awe-struck that the voters sent me here to work in this beautiful building. I read and I am moved by what is written over some of the doors in the Capitol: "We have built no Temple but the Capitol; We consult no common oracle but the Constitution."

What an extraordinary country this is! Its vigor and variety are demonstrated daily in the personalities of the various members of Congress—the different points of view, the different understandings and interests, the variety of accents, even —all these are revealed every day. And to me they are a delight. "We're all here," I say to myself, and that's the way it should be. That there are frustrations daily and disappointments from time to time is certainly true, but it is also true that some of the finest people I have ever known are in the House of Representatives. They work hard. They try to support the public good in a totally disinterested, unselfish way.

Many are extremely gifted. And still the public's opinion of Congress is very low—a matter which is a great concern for all of us and not just for the members.

Oliver Wendell Holmes was writing of the power of truth and its ability to gain acceptance in "the competition of the market. That at any rate," he wrote, "is the theory of our Constitution. It is an experiment, as all life is an experiment." In the midst of all the frustrations and disappointments that work in Congress brings it is comforting to remember that we are still experimenting; that our extraordinary Constitution deliberately provides for an experiment; that although we are clearly not fixed in perfection neither are we locked into inefficiency or corruption.

There are two almost irresistible attractions in a job in Congress. The first is the hope of being useful in bringing about some improvement both in the congressional system itself and in society in general. The second is the opportunity it provides for direct action on behalf of individuals. These are the two faces of elective office—legislation, which is broad and general in scope, and individual cases, which are specific and particular. And it has been my experience that in Congress the second half of the job is the effort to protect the individual against the rules and regulations and, above all, against the indifference of the federal agencies.

There is hardly a facet of life that is now free of some sort of federal action. We take for granted the interest that the Internal Revenue Service has in our affairs, but suppose you are a farmer and decide to raise peanuts; you can't sell your peanuts to be eaten, as peanuts, in America unless you have "an allotment" sanctified by the federal government—a plot of land on which you are permitted to raise peanuts for eating by U.S. citizens.

We have, in fact, worked our way into a veritable web or cocoon of rules and laws. Business, labor, agriculture and the professions are all bound by one set or another. The present trend is to question this situation, which has been built up by accretion over the last hundred years with an enormous burst of regulatory activity in the last fifty. I think most people who have studied the problem would agree that nothing radical can be done quickly. People are used to the conditions and changes must be made carefully, prudently, slowly.

This is probably the biggest lesson I have learned in all my years in the political arena, since Hitler's arrival on the world scene made me aware of the dangers and powers of government. In a system such as ours the point of the exercise is the people. Whenever a legislative body, state or federal, passes a new law or changes an old one there will be an effect in the lives of people who are trying to live down there where theory meets real life. Benevolent intention is not enough, and huge sums of money directed by this intention can often make matters worse. High-rise housing for low-income families is a prime example of the pernicious combination of public funds and ignorant good intentions.

The answer, I think, is to care most sincerely about those one is trying to help, to work with a little more prudence and humility before taking any action that will affect the lives and welfare of other people or change the conditions and arrangements of society in general. We cannot act on the basis of demographic charts and statistics alone; we must start with practical, concrete experience of the needs of people and of existing conditions—whether social or economic—that any legislation might change.

The lesson is that caring is not enough. Intelligence is not enough. Common sense, even—that rarest of all virtues—is not enough. One needs all these and more before there is any hope of bringing wisdom to the affairs of human beings. The Greeks wrote "that wisdom comes alone through suffering . . . against our very will, even in our own despite, comes wisdom by the awful grace of God." Lincoln, more simply, said, "To do the right as God gives us to know the right." I believe that many members of Congress think of this every day.

Remember, you will never arrive at the solution, but you are never absolved from the responsibility of trying.

—THE ETHICS OF THE FATHERS

Part 1

FREEDOM
AND SELF-DISCIPLINE

A country where man recognizes no
check upon his freedom becomes a
country where freedom is the posses-
sion only of the savage few.

—JUDGE LEARNED HAND

"As It Was in the Beginning"

Inevitably, we go back to our beginnings—to the men of the Revolution who sacrificed so much for the freedom we have inherited: Jefferson, whose beloved Monticello was sold for debt; Hamilton, who died bankrupt; Richard Stockton, who signed the Declaration of Independence for New Jersey, was caught by the British, contracted tuberculosis in prison and died of it at the age of 51; John Hart, another New Jersey signer, a farmer from Pennington, said to be illiterate, who came back home to find his wife dead, his stock killed, and his barns burned, who died a ruined man.

And Washington. We tend to forget in our respect and enthusiasm for Jefferson's intellectual brilliance the figure of Washington, whose unshakable qualities of fortitude and tenacity guaranteed the high words and vaulting dreams of the others. Jefferson himself paid tribute to his essential importance: "North and South will hang together if they have you to hang to."

The question we should ask ourselves is not only what made those men able to write such documents as the Declaration and the Constitution—what vision moved them, what education or dreams inspired them—but also what strengths of character and quality made it possible for them to carry these high words and thoughts into action, so that they expressed these ideals not only with their lips, but in their lives.

Undoubtedly, they knew the Bible well. Jefferson read Blackstone and the classics, both Greek and Latin, and Madison probably studied them, too, with John Witherspoon at Princeton. But as far as government itself is concerned, perhaps it is Pericles, the leader of Athens in 430 B.C., whose words can be traced most clearly.

In his famous oration for the dead who fell in battle, Pericles spoke of the difference between Athens and Sparta, ". . . standing on a high platform so that he might be heard by as many people as possible in the crowd," as Thucydides described him. He compared the freedom of a democracy, with its consequent and inevitable lack of discipline, to the regimentation of a totalitarian society, its secrecy and distrust of foreigners.

Speaking of "the glory of Athens," Pericles said: "Everyone is equal before the law; when it is a question of putting one person before another in positions of public responsibility, what counts is not membership of a particular class, but the actual ability which the man possesses." And, further, "We will give our obedience to those we put in positions of authority . . . obey the laws themselves, especially those for the protection of the oppressed, and those unwritten laws which it is an acknowledged shame to break."

The sentences are harmonious and portray the complex system of balances by which democracy is made to work. Equality before the law is balanced by the recognition of individual excellence; liberty is balanced by order, through obedience to laws both written and unwritten.

This system, which allows for the disorder of dissent, relying on self-discipline and consensus to sustain the social structure, needs people who love and understand it. It does not so easily enlist the passion of mindless enthusiasts as do the dictatorships, which throw all constitutional guarantees of orderly process into a bonfire of emotion on behalf of an imposed order.

"Our love of the beautiful does not lead us to extravagance," Pericles said. "Our love of the things of the mind does not make us soft." And they were not soft. They died in terrible wars, as our men have died at Valley Forge and in the frozen mud of Flanders.

We have inherited a wonderful country and a system of government which has survived severe trials. In 1801, Jefferson denied that "Man cannot be trusted with the government of himself. On the contrary," he said in his inaugural, "I believe this the strongest government on earth." But only 64 years later, Lincoln speaking at Gettysburg of the test of our Civil War said, "Whether any nation, so conceived and so dedicated, can long endure."

We *have* endured, with all the complexities freedom entails; but we must bring to our lives as citizens some of the passion and hope and belief and capacity for self-sacrifice which carried forward, like a wave, the vision we now need to recapture.

Report to the Fifth Congressional District on U.S. Bicentennial Celebration, July 4, 1976

No Leaders, Please!

There are many, both here and abroad, who cry out for a leader, for a chief of state who will capture the imagination of the people, inspire them with strong feelings of devotion. ... Anyone who was around in the 1930s, watching Hitler and Stalin at work, must wonder about this. And even in the 1960s we were able to judge the horrors of the "Cultural Revolution," smilingly presided over by Chairman Mao. How is it that the longing for such activists persists in the face of such evidence? One might have expected that we would have been inoculated against leaders, that we would have started to search for improvement in governmental systems, rather than for charismatic individuals. Bertrand Russell understood this when he said that democratic societies should develop "an immunity to eloquence."

At the moment, in America, we are certainly not the victims of eloquence, but we do want a better sense of direction.

What *should* we do in such times? I think the answer is that we must keep our heads—not insisting upon a solution that looks forceful and shouts our power, nor withdrawing into a "Fortress America" isolationism. We must not clamor for big, dramatic gestures that might be dangerously provocative. ... We should applaud those moves that appear constructive and that seem to lead to a moderate, balanced approach to world problems—such as was shown in the Camp David effort. We should not leap to criticize the President just because it now seems to be the fashion, nor should we hesitate to let him know where we think he has vacillated, as in Iran and Taiwan.

If all this sounds like a plea for a bipartisan foreign policy, perhaps it is. What it certainly is intended to be is a plea for a patriotic sense of responsibility in a very fragile world.

Newsletter, *March 8, 1979*

Get Busy

Last week, we observed the birthday of Abraham Lincoln. The inaction of Congress reminds me of an anecdote which is often mentioned by Lincoln Day speakers. At one time, General George McClellan, then commander of the Union forces, was conducting a waiting campaign. He was so careful to avoid mistakes that he was making little headway. President Lincoln wrote him a letter which said:

> My Dear McClellan . . . If you do not want to use the army, I should like to borrow it for awhile. . . . Yours Respectfully, A. Lincoln.

We in Congress should not conduct a waiting campaign. We have an obligation to do the job before us. That in itself would be the most appropriate tribute to Mr. Lincoln's memory.

If we [in Congress] do not get down to business quickly, we might well find the people saying to us: "If you do not want to use those seats, we should like to borrow them for awhile."

Newsletter, *February 20, 1975*

Stand Up and Be Counted

The subject I had not expected to be questioned about was the "affair" in the House, just before the recess, when Representative Wayne Hays and I had a disagreement about an appropriation bill for House expenditures. This had apparently been reported by the press and aroused interest in the district, so perhaps it would be wise to outline it briefly here. In a large $689-million-dollar appropriation bill proposed by the House Administration Committee of which Representative Hays is chairman, there was a $20-million increase in expenses for members of the House. Representative Armstrong of Colorado proposed an amendment cutting these increases out of the big bill, so they could be voted on separately. Representative Hays rose to oppose the amendment and I rose to support it, feeling that we should not take this furtive, back-door method of increasing our emoluments, but, instead, stand up and justify what expenses were necessary, and be counted in the vote.

This was not a partisan issue. Many fine Democrats supported my position, and encouraged me to speak out. I was not arguing that the increased expenditures were not necessary—we had heard no debate or evidence as to whether or not they were—but I was strongly objecting to the fact that it was all done in a closed committee meeting, without public justification, buried in a big bill of which none of the expenditures were debated.

What was at stake? An increase to 26 trips home for each representative, from 18 per year, with no need to produce ticket stubs or vouchers, and the right to take the cash for unused trips; extra staff, so that each member now can spend $227,000 instead of $205,000 for salaries; two free district-wide mailings a year, adding to the publicity each member already gets at public expense through franked mail privileges, increasing the advantage which Common Cause has drawn attention to, that every incumbent has over every would-be challenger.

But none of this came up in the floor debate. The amendment made no mention of these items. It merely cut them out of the rest of the bill, so that they could be separately considered. Neither did I make any mention of them—I said, in fact, that I was making no judgment as to the need for extra expense appropriations, but was objecting only to the method by which we were to obtain them.

The amendment was met by a threat to strip every Republican committee member in the House of any committee staff whatsoever—"and I have the votes to do it." Representative Hays' remarks were expunged from the Congressional Record, but mine were not. Here they are, verbatim:

"Mr. Chairman, I did not expect, and I am sure that many people in this chamber did not expect, to be threatened or to hear threats on the floor when an amendment is offered in good faith in the hope that it will provide good government. I think we can say that we should vote on items that come before the House specifically. I think that is our duty.

"If we need more staff and more money, more and higher salaries, I think we should be prepared to say so, and vote for them. I think that is what representative government is all about.

"But I certainly do not think that a minority, because it is indeed a small minority, should be threatened with loss of a proper proportion of the committee staffs as we have been by the gentleman in the well. As he said, he has the votes to do it. I do not think that many people in this House, certainly the reform-minded members, those who were elected on reform tickets, can be happy, if that is how the government of the United States is going to be run.

"And may I speak of the traditions of this House to those

members who have been here a great deal longer than I have. I am sure that is not what they expect to hear in this chamber. I am new here, but I have been in the legislature at home. I am not unaccustomed to the parliamentary process. I think we have heard here, today, something for which we are all going to be sorry and ashamed."

It was sad that the amendment was defeated 262 to 148, but, significantly, it was not a partisan vote, 39 Democrats joining 109 Republicans in support of it.

Newsletter, *June 12, 1975*

A Question of Honor

If there is one thing the past years have taught us, it is the importance of a keen and high sense of honor in those who handle our governmental affairs.

The investigations to which public officials and agencies have rightly been subjected have revealed an ugly, cheap attitude toward the conduct of public affairs that is an affront to our country and a bitter element of our Bicentennial. That these revelations were necessary is obvious. We could not absorb indefinitely, in our body politic, the poison of such corruption. That they were salutary is less certain.

There is no doubt that the campaign reform law of 1974, setting up the Federal Election Commission with rules for campaign contributions and reporting, reflected the recognition that reform was necessary. To this extent, some good came out of the shame and outrage that the revelations inspired. But it stopped there and, in some ways, retreated. Regulations of the commission were struck down in both Senate and House in 1975.

When Congress convened in January, an even more fundamental principle was challenged. The question was whether or not a committee of Congress, the House Select Committee on Intelligence, having obtained classified information under a certain agreement, should release its report contrary to that agreement.

The arguments on each side were interesting. Proponents on one side urged release on the ground that, although the report contained classified material, a committee of Congress should not be required to submit any report to anyone in the executive branch. Opponents of release spoke mostly of the need to protect the security of the United States. Only a few spoke of the real issue: Whether or not a committee of Congress that had agreed to a certain procedure was not honor-bound to live by that agreement.

Everyone felt, I believe, that the excesses of the Central Intelligence Agency, which were the subject of the report, were intolerable and should be revealed and stopped. But too few were concerned that Congress should live up to its word, should honor its agreement. The incredible part of it all was that many did not even consider this aspect important.

The question that needs to be asked is how we can handle world affairs in such a climate. A student, graduating from a school of public and international affairs last spring, touched on this in his valedictory address: "How does one study—much less conduct—public and international affairs in the absence of a consideration of morals and ethics?"

How can the public support Congress—and we do need public support—in investigations of this kind, when it is common knowledge that a congressional committee may break its word or leak information contrary to an agreement freely given?

Do we not thereby forfeit our right to truthful testimony from witnesses? Provision for an impasse had been agreed upon, with appeal to the President and eventually to the courts, if national security was claimed. This made the desire to publish at once even more incomprehensible.

The President has now suggested a new way of supervising intelligence activities through the National Security Council and a three-man citizens' board. But I think the public should know what the ground rules are—what principles are guiding the responsible supervisors—and Congress is the body that should make those principles clear.

We must learn to live by our principles in the conduct of governmental affairs. A man's—or woman's—word should be as good as a bond. No one should have to be bottled up in an airtight contract with a penalty clause before one can be sure that an agreement freely entered upon will be honored.

Congress must operate, as did the House Judiciary Committee in its Nixon impeachment proceedings, with humility before the Constitution, refusing to mention the existence of any grand jury information that comes to it, scorning the cheap publicity of leaks. Without this, the public will continue to view its government with skepticism. We will always have those who betray our principles, but it is essential that when this happens it should be recognized for what it is. We must be able to believe again, as Americans were once taught to, that there is something important about "our sacred honor."

The New York Times, *February 23, 1976*

Leaks

Recently a member of Congress was accused of telling a number of people, including the press, about matters which had been discussed in executive session in committee. I don't know enough about the rights or wrongs of this particular story to repeat any name or detail but it raises a very old question: Is it ever right to repeat something you have learned in confidence? I think the answer has to be "As a rule, no; sometimes, and in certain ways, yes."

For the answer to be yes, there are two preconditions. The first is that the subject should be morally, ethically, or politically of extreme importance—something that transcends the usual, and forces one to submit the ordinary concept of honor and straight dealing to a higher law of conscience and patriotism. It would be absurd and disingenuous to apply this principle to a matter involving a petty consideration, such as partisan politics. For example, as a member of a committee one might learn something that would gravely embarrass the opposing political party, but it would be absurd to apply the principle of "the higher law" in such a situation. On the other hand, if one heard—even by hearsay—that a certain governmental agency was making a disease-bearing weapon, it is obviously time for action.

And so we come to the second precondition. The way in which action may be taken without dishonor. A frank discussion with the committee in executive session might be the first step, with a request that the chairman look into it and call a hearing so that direct testimony could be given by a representative of the accused and responsible agency. If the chairman refuses, if there is a reason to believe there is collusion or indifference or neglect on his part or on the part of the committee, it seems to me that in certain extreme matters of security one could go to the speaker or even the president. If this is impossible, in this extreme situation, one could announce to the chairman and the committee that failure to act within a certain time would result in an announcement to the press and public.

What is intolerable, in my view, is to learn certain facts—or allegations—when one is being trusted not to reveal them and then, without a word to those who trusted you, repeat the information "off the record," taking cover under the umbrella of the First Amendment guarantees of the press, never standing up for what one has done. Dishonorable, too, is the revelation of sensational information of less than vital importance, even openly, if one received it in confidence.

Somehow we must have a new concept of what is done in government and everywhere else and what is simply not done—what is dishonorable and what is not. Whoever it is who repeats what goes on in a grand jury investigation is guilty of a dishonorable action, because the one being examined is without counsel, resting on the assurance that the proceedings are secret. The whole grand jury system is impugned when leaks are printed in the press, just as the honor of Congress is damaged if one of the members is found to be guilty of revealing secret information.

The best thing we can do to improve matters is to take any such situation seriously. The worst thing we can do is to pass it over, forget it, bury it somewhere in some committee, as if this kind of thing is the expected, normal operating procedure for politicians in general and members of Congress in particular. A Congress which will allow, without censure, a dishonorable action by one of its members is contributing to the attitude that "In government, anything short of murder is 'just politics,' " which Tom Wicker quoted in one of his columns last month.

Everyone is dismayed by the polls which show the low rating of Congress in the confidence of the public. A clear decision on this ethical question might be the first step up for us.

Newsletter, *July 17, 1975*

Press Vigilance

Now that the primary elections are over, these letters to the Fifth District can be resumed and I am sorry to have such unhappy news to report. There have been allegations and revelations of outrageous behavior on the part of certain members of the House of Representatives, which have further depressed and infuriated the public and saddened every member of the House.

Obviously, steps must be taken to discipline ourselves. Two bills have been introduced and I am a cosponsor of both. The first will bring about a reform I recommended last year: Hereafter, if the bill passes, any emoluments or increases in salary for members of the House will be voted on separately; they will not be buried in an omnibus House Administration Bill, as is the practice now. This will curtail some of the powers of the chairman of the House Administration Committee.

The second bill will provide that, by a majority vote in the House, the Committee on Standards of Official Conduct can be ordered to investigate any member's conduct, or that of any staff member. As matters stand now, six votes in the committee can kill an investigation and the only appeal is to the Rules Committee, where eight members can block any action.

Further, I hope that the next Congress will restore some of the Bolling–Frelinghuysen reforms which were wiped out in January 1975, so that the press and public will know how committee members voted on some of these issues.

And this brings us to the heart of the problem. The press

is quick to report any spicy details of congressional misbehavior—and if they relate to a member's official actions, there is every good reason to expose them—but I do not think the media care enough about a member's voting record on matters of congressional reform.

Who knows which members have supported the Federal Elections Commission, and which joined an overwhelming majority to defeat its reforms? How can the public know, if reporters don't even mention their names? At times, there is even complete silence as to the issue.

And this is how the whole sorry mess is encouraged. It starts in the weaknesses of human nature, feeds on the corruption of power, festers and grows in the silence and anonymity that is given it by a Washington press which has grown too used to the system to be shocked by it.

We have had revelations about the misuse of the travel allowances given to members of the House; allegations about the misuse of federal funds in the hiring of personnel—and these are shocking to the public, as they should be. Arriving here, as a member of the public, knowing no more than anyone who reads the papers and hears the news on radio and TV, I was as amazed and shocked as the public is now. But when, last winter, I mentioned some of the antireform votes to a journalist friend down here, his reaction was, "Oh, Mrs. Fenwick, that's just the boys flexing their muscles."

In the face of such an indulgent, paternal attitude, what can one say? The majority is overwhelmingly powerful, and the temptation to indulge in muscle-flexing is perhaps natural, but the incident should at least be reported as the blow to reform which it really was. Instead, it passed in silence, unnoticed, and so the next step was made easier to take. Spurred by the press, Congress has been quick to investigate the executive departments and that has been a good thing. Now we'll see if we can find the same fervor for the corrections and self-discipline we sorely need.

Newsletter, *June 10, 1976*

Say What You Mean

Events in the past few weeks have produced steadily increasing evidence of a destructive element in the way some of our institutions are developing. It might be described as selective morality, or selective indignation, in some cases; in others, it takes the form of departing from the stated objective of the group—a practice which, if followed to its conclusion in a commercial situation, might well be called (and would be prosecuted as) misleading advertising.

In all cases, the unfortunate trend is toward a certain falsity, a departure from intellectual honesty. "We say this—but," expresses the attitude. Shining exceptions are such groups as the International Red Cross and the League of Women Voters. During the war in Vietnam, members of the Red Cross steadfastly called for inspection of all prisons—both north and south. In New Jersey, when the president of the League, Nina McCall, told me she was running for office, she had so loyally honored the League's stated standards that I had to ask her "In which party?", although we were friends and had worked often together. (She was a Democrat.)

Other groups and individuals are not so scrupulous. The United Nations, both in committee and in the General Assembly, is slipping further and further from its original principles. Ambassador Moynihan has been firm in opposition. He objected to the Assembly's resolution branding Zionism as racist, not only because it damaged the integrity of the UN, but also because it was an outrageous lie. Further, as examples of selective morality, he has drawn attention to two commit-tee resolutions, properly and strongly supported by the United States. His point was that they urged amnesty for political prisoners in Chile and South Africa only.

Newsletter, *December 18, 1975*

Cannons from Left and Right

Everyone in America seems to be joining an organization of some kind, and in Congress one hears from them all. Many are invaluable citizen groups, concerned with good issues, indispensable to the community and the causes they serve. Others are sensible groups which simply want more money spent in one particular field—with cuts, of course, in every other budget. Much smaller in number, but still the fastest-growing category, are the opinion groups—right and left.

An extreme example on the left is a "nonprofit, educational" organization (thereby qualifying for a 1.8-cent mailing rate), which has urged wives to lecture their husbands on the evils of corporations—". . . ask some probing questions of your husband" about "rampant corporate criminality . . . when your husband comes home for dinner this evening." These were some of the suggestions in one mailing. A subsequent mailing from the same group went further and offered a $25,000 reward to secretaries who inform on their high-ranking corporate employees and get them imprisoned for crime.

If it were not so ugly it would be funny. Imagine the atmosphere in an office where half are spies and the rest spied upon; think of the family dinner table conversations if these suggestions are adopted!

In addition to this rather specialized group, there are others on the left in favor of almost every project that costs money, and against any talk about the deficit or the government debt.

On the right there are similar groups. They also send out letters and flyers, and, in addition, they circulate magazines.

In place of attacks against conservative spending practices from the left, we have attacks from the right against any form of international cooperation. When the cry of the left is against "big business," the cry of the right is against "big labor," and against *all* spending for human concerns.

The end result of this passionate one-sided approach to the issues of the day is absurd; ordinary patriotism becomes suspect to the left, as evidence of right-wing extremism; whereas, a concern for constitutionally guaranteed civil rights will brand you as a flaming and dangerous radical in the eyes of the right.

The question this raises is "Why stop there?" If one is not equally concerned about the political prisoners in other countries, it is clear that one is not appealing to a principle, but simply applying a selective political judgment when and where convenient. The principle of human rights, to which appeal is made, is reduced to a politically expedient slogan. Ambassador Moynihan quotes Stephen Spender in this regard: "It came to me that unless I cared about every murdered child indiscriminately, I didn't really care about murdered children at all."

With this in mind, what do we say about the group of officials belonging to an important church organization urging America not to intervene in Angola, ignoring the Cuban government, which has been reliably reported as having 3,000 troops there, and the Soviet government, which is sending heavy armaments? When a church sends money for medical supplies to the Angola battlefront, should it not go to all three factions? Does it not become a political gesture if it goes only to one?

The citizens of this country give tax-deductibility to certain groups for certain specific reasons: that the groups are dedicated to religious, educational, charitable or civic purposes, according to their names. But is this not being abused when the tax-deductibility properly granted to one organization is being "loaned" to another group, which has no tax-deductible status and is frankly lobbying for or against specific legislation before the Congress?

Is there not an element of falsity when an organization which requests funds from the public as being "nonpartisan," or "bipartisan," consistently and almost exclusively favors one political party rather than another? Are all citizens comfortably sure that an investigating committee of Congress will issue a report that is devoid of political bias?

It is difficult to see how we can correct these abuses, and they exist in various ways and in varying degrees in other fields as well. As Consumer Affairs Director in New Jersey, I was in charge of the Bureau of Charities Registration, under a law requiring reports from all organizations collecting more than $10,000 a year from the public. To my dismay, I discovered that one group had collected $44,000, spent $32,000 on administration, $2,500 on dues to the national organization, and about $1,000 for the supposed beneficiaries, and had banked the rest of the money.

There may be many such practices all over the country, and I have asked Chairman Ullman of the Ways and Means Committee to consider how the public can be protected from such an abuse. Perhaps the best way would be to require that givers be informed as to what proportion of the money collected is spent on each category. "Truth in Asking" might be the answer to this.

No group or individual can conform to the highest possible standard, every day, on every issue. It is the trend that is worrying, and the first step toward reversing the trend is to recognize it.

Newsletter, *December 18, 1975*

One longs for a voice in the middle, and the mail often brings such balanced and refreshing views. In fact, the overwhelming majority of those who write me belong to this sensible persuasion—able to see a little right and a little wrong on both sides of many questions.

And now we have evidence of the same commendably balanced point of view in the latest report of the Inter-American Human Rights Commission of the Organization of American States. This commission has done valuable work in publishing violations of human rights in Chile, including reports of summary imprisonment and even torture.

These reports have been widely circulated for some time and have properly aroused a great deal of attention and concern. Now comes an 83-page commission report on conditions in Cuba. The difficulties in making the report were even greater than those experienced in Chile, because the commission was denied permission to visit the island.

The action of the commission in issuing this second report is important for many reasons. We need more people and organizations in a position to bring the public objective and honest reporting which is clearly neither self-serving, nor at the service of any particular ideology, nor the product of a passionately held—rather than a reasonable—point of view. We need people who care about the truth and are not reaching for every fact that supports their position, avoiding every other.

We also need organizations which are doing what the public thinks they're doing. Some, which claim a nonpartisan position, are not nonpartisan at all, but demonstrably biased toward one party or another. Some businesses adopt names which suggest a charitable purpose, when they are in fact profitable businesses, registered as such.

If we claim to be interested in starving children, as Stephen Spender wrote, we must be concerned about *all* starving children, wherever they live. If we are champions of human rights, we must be willing to recognize violations wherever they are found. Selective indignation is not convincing; it defeats its own purpose to persuade. Intelligent opinions and decisions need calm and reasonable exposition of the facts —not bombardments of emotion.

There are cannons to left of us and cannons to right of us. I only wish Congress were more like the "noble six hundred" who marched unflinchingly forward through the barrages from each side.

Newsletter, *June 24, 1976*

The Power of the Public

When Arthur Burns was chairman of the Federal Reserve, he used to send me copies of his speeches asking for comments. Over and over again, in these very erudite and, I must say, difficult to read speeches on economics and Federal Reserve actions, I was struck by the fact that the most common words were expectation, perception, and confidence. Those were the words. What do people believe? What do they expect? And this is going to influence economics almost as much as any other factor.

Everything depends on the consensus in the country as to what kind of standards we're going to live by. Everything depends on the expectations as to what kind of economy we're going to have. And it reminded me of a dinner party long ago when I asked a bank president how big a national debt could be? This was in the early fifties. I thought the answer would be ten times the Gross National Product (GNP) divided by the ratio of something, but his answer was simply, "As large as public confidence will support." That's it.

There you are. Economics is not a science, in the sense that a policy can be repeatedly applied under similar conditions and will repeatedly produce similar results. It won't. Because you may deal in one place with a people who have perceptions and expectations so different from another's. There's no sure thing. We don't know enough. Maybe the most important people of our coming generation are going to be psychologists. If only we could find individuals like Arthur Burns and Elmer Staats, the latter of the General Accounting Office. They were recognized and admired by everyone because they never tried to make a point or do anything, but just to tell you what they believed to be true! The big temptation is to bolster one's own position and that exists wherever there are human beings. It doesn't make any difference whether you're talking about a university or a Congress.

Years ago, I had an interesting conversation with the head of the School of International Law at Columbia. We got into some kind of a disagreement. I can't remember exactly what the difference between us was, but finally I asked him in exasperation, "Well, then, what *is* the law?"

And he said, "Law is crystallized public opinion. That's all. Crystallized public opinion."

And I think perhaps he was right. Sometimes a law goes beyond what public opinion will support. And when you get that, you get odd votes from the jury. They know that the penalty is heavier than they want to be associated with, and so they won't vote "guilty." I saw it happen. A great big 18-year-old had beaten up a poor old lady in a New Jersey town. He should have been judged guilty, but a very heavy penalty was involved and the jury acquitted him. Later I asked one of the jury, "How could you ever judge that boy innocent?"

"Well, the penalty was so heavy," the juror replied.

If we get mandatory death sentences, we're going to have happy murderers walking the streets in droves, because juries won't convict. We must base law on a consensus, and that is why I think the group that's going to be in the ascendancy may be the psychologists. We need to hear ego-free, bias-free, honest, recognized voices such as Elmer Staats or Arthur Burns.

Taped interview, November 20, 1980

Shadow and Substance

Last Sunday night, back in the District, an ecumenical group gave a dinner for me. It was headed by a rabbi and a banker and a committee including a Roman Catholic priest from Dunbarton Priory and a Protestant Episcopal minister. They invited Henry Kissinger to speak. I found it very touching.

I knew a lot of the people there. The room was crowded. Of course, they came to hear Henry. The purpose of all this was to start a Fenwick Forest in Israel, and Kissinger spoke, with that strange, slow, rather caressing voice I've always considered one of his main charms. He has a brilliant mind and his speech was very fair, not attacking the present administration, not partisan, hoping for a bipartisan foreign policy. I was impressed by his fine, high-minded talk.

But then the rabbi spoke, quoting from Thoreau and Montaigne and the Bible. He's a magnificent speaker and it was inspiring. Henry's was a fine speech: tactical, strategic, global, geo-political, current, forceful, brilliant. But the rabbi was talking about the roots, the springs, of our civilization. Why we hope for what we hope for, why we value what we value, why we seek a just and merciful and compassionate society.

It was absolutely fascinating. It was so different a speech from the other. I kept thinking of Solzhenitsyn and Sakharov, also so different in mind. There they were side by side, in the Somerville Inn, in Somerset County, New Jersey.

We must have both, I believe. We must have somebody who speaks to eternal verities, if we can discern what they possibly might be, or at least, to the ancient values. And then we need someone who can apply them in the modern context.

What's so awful about this century, honestly, is that the more we learn in the way of technology, and the more we master mysteries in space and air waves and atoms, in chemicals and ocean depths the worse it gets. Consider communications. What are we communicating? What fruits are there? Brotherhood? Understanding? International good will? There are voices which speak to this. Here is one of them:

> We have grasped the mystery of the atom and neglected the Sermon on the Mount. The world has achieved brilliance without wisdom, power without conscience. Ours is a world of nuclear giants and ethical infants. We know more about war than we do about peace, more about killing than we know about living.— General Omar N. Bradley

It is strange—but comforting—to see that a man trained and hardened in the harshest element of modern times—the substance of politics—can evoke so eloquently the verities of which the rabbi spoke.

Taped interview, February 4, 1980

The People Have Spoken

These newsletters, suspended on the Fourth of July out of respect for my opponents in the election, will be resumed now that the election is over. And what an amazing event it was! With Republicans in charge in the White House, and in the majority in the Senate for the first time in 26 years, it will be a time of testing for the victors. We have been in the minority for so long—and are still a minority in the House—that we have forgotten what it is like to be more nearly responsible for the conduct of our country's affairs.

It is clear, I believe, what the voters want us to do: end inflation; increase employment opportunities; develop workable programs to make us more energy-independent; increase productivity; get our defense establishment in order. These are the practical problems, but there is perhaps something else which accounts for such a vote, an intangible "feeling" that a whole new approach is needed.

A poet wrote, "For each age is an age that is dying and one that is coming to birth." And that is what we are seeing. The people feel—and I think rightly—that the problems we wanted to solve (and still want to solve) cannot be addressed as they have been. Too many loose ends, too many scandals year after year in the same very expensive programs, uncorrected as far as the public can see, while the taxes get heavier and heavier, and the problems get worse.

Intelligent Democrats have seen this as clearly as any Republican. Earlier this year, Paul Tsongas, junior Senator from Massachusetts and a Democrat, outlined the need for new solutions in a most important speech at a meeting of the

Americans for Democratic Action. But habits are hard to change. Large expensive programs were always seen as proof of benevolence and vision. They were also a proven way to get reelected. The enormous strength and wealth of the economy seemed able to support this system so it went on and on, increasing the national debt from $274 billion in 1955 to $908 billion in 1980, raising the cost of debt service from $4.8 billion to $64.5 billion in the same period.

Any attempts to slow the rise were met by accusations of "balancing the budget on the backs of the poor." Attempts to stop the "fraud, abuse, and mis-management," which were routinely reported by the General Accounting Office (GAO) and the Inspectors General, were met by vague reassurances from the various departments that corrections were being made and—far more importantly—by complete indifference on the part of the chairmen of the congressional committees in charge of the enabling legislation.

It is no wonder, therefore, that voters became increasingly restive—suspicious, skeptical, uneasily aware that they were on a treadmill that might lead to disaster, with no confidence in the ability or desire of those in charge to change direction.

Defense programs which had cost $1.817 trillion in the period from 1955 to 1980 resulted in a situation which made it impossible in 1980 for a navy ship to leave Newport News because its complement of noncommissioned officers was incomplete. Programs designed to help the cities and the very poor, which cost $2.438 trillion in that time, have resulted in a situation now described as "more desperate than ever" and "an invitation to revolution" by respected officials of nationwide organizations. The system obviously was not working.

Now all of us who have been elected or reelected must face up to the task we have been handed. We must listen to those who are not only informed and expert but also concerned and sensible. The difficulty comes in the fact that equally distinguished authorities—in all fields, but especially economics—differ violently as to the appropriate remedies. Oddly enough, even in economics, which one might expect to be relying on facts and figures, a dominant and recurring theme is the use of words such as "confidence" and "expectation." What the public believes, or feels, or perceives is almost as important as any other factor.

Yes, we must listen and study but perhaps the spirit in which we face the questions before us is what matters most. King Solomon asked Almighty God for wisdom and understanding to rule his people. Lincoln wrote of "doing the right as God gives us to know the right." The difficulties we are experiencing are man-made—not earthquakes or hurricanes. And it seems impossible that we cannot improve the situation if we approach it with the proper zeal and spirit.

Newsletter, *November 10, 1980*

Why I Am a Republican

I can tell you exactly why I am a Republican. When I was a young woman, Hitler was elected (by over 80 percent of the vote, as I remember) in one of the most literate countries of the world, by a people preeminent in music, science, and many other fields. And the government of that country proceeded to exercise the most cruel injustices against many of its people. Some who had fought for Germany in the First World War were treated like criminals, or worse, only because of their race or religion. It struck me as a hideous perversion of what government is meant to be—an institution designed to bring about a just society.

Since then, I have never really trusted government and it is because I don't trust government that I am a Republican. Most of my family were—and are—Democrats, particularly in the older generation, and I have noticed that this trust, or lack of trust, is what divides us.

A good Republican, I think, is as sensitive to the suffering of others as anyone else, but a first reaction would be "Let's get together and do something," not "The government must take charge of this." When there is no way of organizing relief apart from government, Republicans are as quick as Democrats to turn to government for help, as can be proved by the impetus Republicans and Republican administrations have given to government programs. But the general trend of Republican thinking (it cannot perhaps be called a philosophy or ideology) is to move toward private, volunteer, or religious action as a first step.

A good Democrat, on the other hand, takes solid satisfaction in setting up a good big government program: a new department in Washington, perhaps, with a secretary and deputy assistant secretaries, regional directors and deputy directors, and all the offices, outreach agencies, statisticians, and employees that a good big program, in their view, really deserves.

Good Democrats don't mind mandatory laws, regulations, and ordinances, nor do they object, as a rule, to measures that prohibit citizens to do certain things. Good Republicans tend to ask "Why? Is the situation such that we must order people around like that?"

It's a different point of view and I believe it is the basic difference between a Republican and a Democrat. And it goes further, of course, into the question of the individual versus the whole of society. Republicans believe that the strength of individual initiative and motivation will produce ever-widening choices and greater freedom; they try to encourage opportunities for choice. Democrats are more concerned that government should organize in such a way as to make individual choice—with all its chances for mistake and failure—less important. A Republican speaks of "Freedom to . . ."; a Democrat of "Freedom from . . ."I'm a Republican.

Written in response to a question from Newsday, *for a pre-1980 Election edition.*

Voluntarism

Of all the characteristics of American society, one of the most valuable and typical is the spirit of voluntarism. The spirit is far more important than its practical effects, essential though these are. Where would our New Jersey towns and villages be without our volunteer fire and first aid and rescue squads? Could our hospitals manage without volunteer aides? Could the Red Cross meet emergencies without them?

These are just some of the best known and most obvious practical effects, but underlying them is the spirit that makes people do such things. Tired men and women who have worked all day spend long evenings as Board of Education members, Council or Township Committee members, wrestling with hometown problems. They serve on Health Boards, Recreation Commissions, Nursing Boards, art and cultural associations—all working without compensation of any kind. And the list is much longer than this.

The wonderful spirit of responsibility and human solidarity that these activities epitomize is the binding force of our nation. It is the lifeblood of communities, bringing people together in shared and disinterested work for the common good. We see it in the school children, for example, who come as volunteers to our veterans' hospitals, "adopting" a patient, remembering birthdays and Christmas with a card. And we see it, too, in people such as this volunteer—a nurse in the *First* World War—who came every week to Lyons Hospital. I saw her there in the summer of 1976 and she had come, faithfully, every year since anyone could remember.

And yet, still more is needed. The scattering of families and the complexity of modern life mean that more and more services are needed. We must be sure that every blind person has someone willing to read the weekly mail, to provide transportation to a meeting once a month. We must be sure that every isolated, elderly, and lonely person gets a telephone call every day, at a stated time, to check if everything is all right. Handicapped people need help such as that now provided by about sixty couples in our district through the Somerset County Unit for Retarded Citizens. The Voluntary Action Center of Morris County places volunteers in 250 agencies throughout the county—just to cite two of the many. And still there are gaps to be filled.

The question is how these needs are going to be met. It is intolerable to think of blind people without help, but if volunteers don't rally around, something will have to be done. It is also true that so much has been—and is being—done by government that the volunteer spirit is not encouraged. I remember some years ago, when I was testifying on behalf of tenants in Newark's Central Ward high-rise public housing, I met a fine citizen who was famous among his fellow citizens in the ward for his disinterested and vigorous service on their behalf. He told me then: "I have a job. I wouldn't touch government money—federal money is poison."

I knew what he meant. Service to the community given as a volunteer is one thing; a government job, however honorably and faithfully held, is different.

What we must accept, I think, is that there are dozens of desirable services a compassionate and alert mind can identify. But it is simply impossible to believe that every desirable program can be funded with tax money. The end is in sight. We must use heart and head to work out a developed volunteer system—recognized and honored.

Walt Whitman in his *Pioneers, O Pioneers* wrote of the courage and heart of those who moved by their own initiative. That same spirit must move us to invent and improvise and work to do what needs to be done. Schools and churches and temples can help; unions and business organizations can encourage this sort of enterprise and they do. At a recent meeting concerned with the education of handicapped children, it was wonderful to hear the announcement of a joint effort of labor, industry, and teachers to make a properly equipped therapeutic playroom.

These are the ways we must follow and encourage. The red tape that public money necessarily brings in its train can be avoided while expense is spared and the good will that warms life and makes a community out of strangers is multiplied many times.

Newsletter, *February 9, 1978*

The Case for Volunteers

My last report was about "self-help"—voluntarism—as a substitute for some tax-supported but highly desirable programs. I had not realized, until I read a subsequent editorial in *The New York Times,* that I was touching on such a delicate and timely subject, with an immediate application far beyond the Fifth District of New Jersey.

I suggested, as you may remember, that genuine concern for human problems, expressed in action, could supplement (and in some cases do more than) the tax-supported programs we have all become so accustomed to.

The editorial in the newspaper, and an accompanying news report, were concerned with the extraordinary response provoked by Mayor Beame's recent appeal for volunteers in New York City. Usually, there were ten calls a day at City Hall, offering services, but as soon as he called for volunteers to help keep city services operating in the face of the city's financial crisis, there were hundreds of such calls.

Specifically, the editorial was concerned with a problem in public libraries, which have done such magnificent work for the people of New York, and were being cut back in services owing to the financial crisis. According to *The Times,* efforts of the citizen-volunteers were met with "frustrations . . . because of the stubborn refusal of the librarians' union, and Public Library trustees, to sanction the use of willing volunteers. . . ." This particular problem was solved "through injection of federal funds."

As the editorial pointed out, this is not the proper, long-term solution of the problem. The people need services the city cannot pay for. There are volunteers ready to help and they should be allowed to do so.

Unions are an essential part of our economic life. If we didn't have honest, efficient unions, concerned with the welfare of their members, we would have to have even more government laws and regulations—rigid, unsuited perhaps to any specific industry or business—and no one would want to see that.

In addition, I think everyone accepts the fact that jobs cannot be eliminated lightly. People have to live. Enlightened self-interest suggests the solution—attrition—used by many industries where mechanization has enabled the company to remain competitive, without anyone losing a job. As employees retire, or decide to leave, changes are made, and new machinery—or volunteers—may be introduced.

On the other hand, we cannot accept a solution which says, "If the taxes can't cover those services, they must be eliminated." Taxes simply cannot cover everything we would like to have. Enlightened union leaders know this. Edward Swayduck, in 28 years as president of the Lithographers' Union—an occupation outstanding in technological improvements and inventions—never had a strike. Labor-saving devices were absorbed by attrition, with shared profits. In public service, there are no profits to share, but there are other considerations. The main one is that the public—the hardworking tax-paying citizen who supports the whole structure—must be served.

We must move with concern for all the people involved in such situations—union members and public alike—but we cannot accept a "stubborn refusal" and more "federal funds" as the only way out of every such impasse.

Newsletter, *March 11, 1976*

On Violence

We have seen in our own country the attempted assassination of our President and the wounding of three brave men who tried to protect him. And as a menacing sequel, the outrageous attack on His Holiness Pope John Paul II.

Violence has concerned many of us for a long time. In September 1980, I wrote the following for a newspaper in the district:

Day after day, by newspaper, radio, and television, new reports of violence come in from every corner of our nation and the world. It is heartbreaking to think of the suffering the reports suggest: the children bombed in their nurseries, the fathers of families shot as they go to work. But these reports make us wonder, too, at the cause of all this and the possible remedies.

Some have held that communications are part of the problem, that ideas for new and more efficient violence can be spread, like a terrible disease, in the printed—and, even more, the heard—words, and the photographed action. However true this may be, it suggests no cure because the reports can never be stopped; censorship is no answer. In fact, to the contrary, we need more information, not less. The important question is why these grisly events seem to stimulate more violence, rather than a sense of horror and revulsion.

The only answer seems to be the public's reaction. It starts with the misapplication of the virtue of tolerance; as long as the public continues to condone violence whenever an altruistic motive is claimed, we will continue to see violence grow. We have seen it in our own country and, even more conspicuously, in foreign countries. Surely we must ask what is happening when in Iran for the first time in any Muslim country in hundreds of years, people are stoned to death by the authorities as punishment for crime. How can the public tolerate such a thing? Another frightful spectacle was Uganda, where for eight years the people suffered mass murders, as they did in Cambodia. Idi Amin in Africa and Pol Pot in Asia —these are extreme examples of government outrages but what do we say of the heads of state who prepare and finance assassination? These heads of state are not outlawed in the United Nations. They are not discredited as they should be. On the contrary, the United Nations even welcomed Arafat, complete with gun. In our times, significantly, the three outstanding voices against violence have been silenced by murder—Mahatma Gandhi in India, Archbishop Romero in El Salvador, and Dr. Martin Luther King, here at home.

We should consider violence here, where as citizens we have responsibility and ways of action not available to all others. We have opened the door to all violence here, I believe, by condoning certain violent acts, particularly when no selfish gain is apparent and an unselfish reason is claimed. For example, were we as concerned as we should have been when anti-Vietnam War protestors broke into Selective Service Centers and destroyed vital records? Are we now as concerned as we should be when demonstrators break down the fences at nuclear power plants? Do we move at once to arrest people who attack other people in political or labor confrontations? The answer in all cases is no. At a conference studying the causes of violence, I once heard a clergyman—and this is hard to believe—say that violence had to be condoned and accepted in certain situations, "although I would not commit violence myself." He called it "liberation theology."

Since this point of view is not uncommon, perhaps we should not be surprised that violence grows. Against it, our main defense is our traditional respect for a rule of law. We must uphold legal rights and protect them always, because it is only if we insist on the right of free speech for all our people, the right to assemble peacefully, to publish and petition, that we can with equal conviction move against those who commit violence. It is our Constitutional duty, for example, to grant licenses for peaceful demonstrations on behalf of even the most unpopular causes. But, surely, those who abuse respect for their rights by breaking the law should be made to feel the full weight of public opinion against them, and receive the appropriate penalty.

Vandalism is the first face of violence and an increasing problem, locally as well as nationally. It is without excuse, motive, or reason. It is violence against property, and it grows daily, feeding on a certain indifference in the public. In one municipality in the Fifth District young vandals tore out the porch railings on one of the town's few historic buildings, and did it again when the railings were repaired. In another municipality, also in the Fifth District, police cars are being battered and overturned, and windows are being broken every week. Such vandalism, all too common in our cities, is often blamed on poverty, unemployment, overcrowding, and other similar misfortunes. But the police chief in one of our loveliest country villages, deploring the continual depredations of young vandals, told me that he attributed the cause to "too much family affluence." He felt that parents were too often absent in pursuing their own pleasures and that this encouraged vandalism through family indifference.

To sum up, we ask what we can do. I think the answer is that all of us—citizens, parents, legislators, everyone—must decide that it is necessary finally to draw a line. With full respect for our Constitutional rights and those of others, we must make it clear that violence and vandalism, no matter what excuse may be given, are going to be met with the firm disapproval of the public, and with all the appropriate penalties of the law.

These were the thoughts of September 1980, and they are a pale forerunner of the feelings all of us share now. An attack on the head of a great nation, followed by the attempted murder of a great spiritual leader—how do we react to these facts? We must start by understanding what is happening. We are witnessing, I believe, one of the unexpected consequences of worldwide, instant communication. We have not understood all its implications or prepared ourselves for its possible effects. Now we must strengthen ourselves in our innermost reactions. Starting at home, children should hear their parents express anger at violent deeds, pity and shame for the violators of the peace and their families. The community should reflect the same spirit, as should our judges in their decisions and remarks. The professors in our universities and colleges should take another look at some of their lectures and those of their colleagues, knowing that the right of academic freedom demands an increased sense of responsibility and that they—rightly—have no other censorship than their own.

There are undoubtedly other views of this outbreak of worldwide violence and other, better, ways of trying to change the course of events, but it is surely the duty of all of us to start thinking about the full meaning of the events we are witnessing.

Newsletter, *May 27, 1981*

The Limits of Protest

What we must have is a consensus in this country, a consensus on lawbreaking but especially on violence. The world is turning itself inside out in this regard. It's just absolutely awful. I think, one of the reasons is that we started not exactly praising, but certainly condoning violence. When you pleaded a noble cause, violence was "understood." And we killed the voices of non-violence: Gandhi was murdered. Archbishop Romero was murdered. Dr. Martin Luther King was murdered. Now, Dr. Martin Luther King taught us something about civil disobedience in the Thoreau tradition. He camped in a southern town near the courthouse. You're not allowed to camp near the courthouse, and that's a good rule. You don't want mobs intimidating a jury. But he camped there for the night. He knew he was breaking the law but he wanted to publicize his cause. When he was picked up, uncomplaining, he went to jail and paid the penalty, which he approved of.

That's civil disobedience. No property was damaged. They all cleaned up the place. There was no violence. But we now have terrorism. We have condoned people who were "antiwar," against the Vietnam War, breaking into Selective Service offices and putting blood on the records. We have condoned anti-nuclear people breaking down the fences of nuclear plants. We have condoned demonstrations where there's violence, whether it's labor or political.

When I was in the Middle West lecturing for the book I wrote for *Vogue,* they told me about the labor people trying to get a small company's workers to join the Teamsters. "The workers" were a father and son. They beat up the father because he said, "It's just my son and me. I don't really employ anybody. We just have these two trucks." He was beaten and disabled. So the son began driving the trucks, and he was so badly beaten that he lost an eye. This happened when I was in Grand Rapids, Michigan.

Now, that's an outrage, and I don't care what the reasons were. Anybody who does that to another human being should be in jail. At the Holland Tunnel, drivers were dragged off their trucks. No one has a right to do that.

We've got to do two things. We've got to have a clear understanding that rights are inviolable and violence and vandalism are outrageous. We must allow peaceful protest, peaceful demonstrations, the right to speak and publish and assemble. We can't be arrested for what we say. All our rights have to be guaranteed. When the Nazis planned that disgraceful march in Skokie, Illinois, I think the ACLU was absolutely right. It was a wicked thing to do. It was cruel. Ham Fish and I were organizing members of Congress who would have gone up, had they marched, to march behind them saying, "This is a disgraceful and cruel thing to do." We had a right to demonstrate, too. And that's how it must be. We must stand up for the most unpopular causes, upholding their rights. Otherwise we're lost. We must stand up for the rights of the Ku Klux Klan and the Nazis and the Communists when they want to have a demonstration, and they behave peacefully. We must stand up for them. Otherwise we have no right to insist on the penalty, when the Berrigan brothers go up and smash a missile as they did the other day. They had no right to break into a company's office, and take a hammer and break up a missile. That was disgusting. And I don't care who they are. They are human beings and they have their rights as priests and human beings, but they certainly deserve the full penalty of the law.

Taped interview, September 19, 1980

A Sense of Injustice

I have come to believe that one thing people cannot bear is a sense of injustice. Poverty, cold, even hunger, are more bearable than injustice. If you feel that the deck's stacked against you—that the very organs of the state which are supposed to be protecting you are against you, that your taxes are not giving you equal protection—if it's all loaded against you, it's unbearable.

What is reported as the cause of the Miami riots, as being at the bottom of the resentment? Injustice, injustice!

Woodrow Wilson said, "The business of government is justice." No wonder that justice, even in the time of the Bible, was recognized as the great principle.

I was not surprised by the Newark riots in 1967 because I had been in Newark, listening to the people there, hearing their complaints about the courts and the police. When the riots finally came and 26 people were dead, I was not taken by surprise. It was a terrible thing. Terrible. And later, in Plainfield, a policeman was stomped to death—literally, people jumping up and down until he was dead. A sense of injustice was the root of these riots. If you listen to people you can feel the rising sense of injustice, the warning of a storm to come.

Taped interview, September 19, 1980

Ultimate Betrayal

Mr. Speaker, members of the House, we have heard today eloquent statements concerning the barbaric assassination of the former prime minister and head of his party in a free country. I have family in Italy, and this matter is very close to my heart.

It is, indeed, barbaric and terrible that such a distinguished and innocent person should have been held prisoner and finally assassinated in a cruel, long drawn-out agony, but I would like to remind the members of the House that it is not just a prime minister who was killed by this vicious Red Brigade. Five policemen lost their lives when he was taken, one after another. A sergeant was shot in Milan, because he was going to be able to give some evidence. In that country people are being killed every day.

It is nationwide, and it is happening to simple, ordinary people. The extortion and blackmail are not confined to just the very rich. A little shopkeeper in the southern part of Italy had $1,000 extorted from him when they kidnaped his child.

Terrorism is something we are all going to have to be aware of. It is rising in the world, vicious terrorism under the so-called justification of political action. We have not been careful enough about it. We have not been clear enough in our response. Wrong is wrong, and it should not take a prime minister's death to show us that. One policeman's death ought to be enough.

Congressional Record, *May 11, 1978*

A Sad Story

Mr. Speaker, last week another diplomat, at his post in Geneva, Switzerland, fell victim to assassination. This time it was a Turkish diplomat, the latest in a list that includes 19 Turkish diplomats and their wives and children murdered since 1973.

And so the sad story continues. Terrorists in every corner of the world, claiming one cause or another as justification, have made murder an all too usual political comment. There is no answer, perhaps, except in the hearts of human beings. No religion seems to be able to stamp out violence. No law seems to reach or discourage those who bomb day-care centers and marketplaces, who kill policemen and magistrates on their way to work, businessmen in their offices.

It seems to begin with the feeling that a cause that seems noble is reason enough to break the law, to violate personal or property rights. Until we get this clear, until we draw a straight line between lawful dissent and assembly on the one hand, and illegal assaults on persons or abuse of property on the other hand, we will never stamp out, at the source, the long ugly trail that leads in its extreme form to murder itself.

Congressional Record *June 18, 1981*

Part 2

THE BUSINESS
OF GOVERNMENT

The business of government is justice.
—Woodrow Wilson

Ways and Means

The members of Congress work harder than I ever believed as a member of the general public, but we don't always work well. We sometimes lose sight of the ends, the purpose of the whole exercise of government, in a preoccupation with means. And sometimes we lose sight of the means; the purpose is good, we say, without stopping long enough to make sure some injustice is not done along the way.

Our young people—students, specifically—have again this spring, as they did last May, given me a lesson on the subject. And with the lesson, great hope and encouragement. In both cases the occasion was a college commencement. In both cases, the happy surprise came from the valedictorian's address, which was concerned with precisely the same subject as my own.

Last May, at Stevens Institute of Technology in Hoboken, the subject was the need for synthesis, the absolute necessity for the various disciplines (engineering, economics, sociology, psychology—all of them) to consult, or at least to consider, the state of the art beyond each scholar's special field. A planner working with demographic charts will not produce something useful if the city planned for that blank space on the map turns out to be placed over a valuable aquifer; the hydrologist should have been consulted. The urbanologist who makes a truly practical plan for urban living will have consulted a psychologist competent to advise on stress and crowding. And so it would be for each subject: Economics should be joined with politics and sociology to devise a plan that stands a chance of being voted into action; chemistry must work with ecology before a new weed or pest killer is launched. And finally, the question—perhaps emphasized a little more strongly in my address than in the student's—is whether or not all of those subjects should not be studied and developed by those who have some knowledge of philosophy and theology. It seems doubtful that we can develop the kind of society that gives satisfaction to human beings if we ignore the study of themes which deal with some of our highest and most basic aspirations, needs and, impulses—whether conscious or subconscious.

This May's happy surprise came at the graduation exercises of the School of Public and International Affairs at George Washington University. The honor student evaluated and praised the courses he had been given and the professors who gave them. But he ended his address with a plea for a wider discussion of ethics and morality. "How can public or international affairs be studied or understood, much less implemented, if moral values are ignored?" was the point of his closing words.

My own short speech had been planned to pose the same question, based on Archibald Cox's statement, "I know what I admire, what I hope I would always do," ending with the wisdom that comes through experience, "But as I grow older I know how hard it is to be sure that I can say 'That I would never do!' " The humility of the final clause is probably the beginning of wisdom, but surely the first step comes in thrashing out, step by step, what each one of us truly admires.

At this point, I am sure everyone has understood that a good part of my pleasure in these two events comes from the thought that the generation gap doesn't work all the time. It was an enormous satisfaction to discover that the students and I were thinking about the same things and coming to much the same conclusions. But the importance to me was the direction of their thinking, which coincided, incidentally, with the honor student's address at the high school in my home town of Bernardsville, also this May. There we were told that study should not be tied to marks or acclaim but, rather, to the pure pursuit of knowledge for its own sake and as a means of helping others. The moral and ethical values the Washington student called for were already being decided upon by the high school student in New Jersey.

Surely, all this indicates that there is less preoccupation with material success, which so many criticized in the past, and less emphasis on security, which has come in for more recent criticism. There is no hint of "Stop the World, I want to get off" which characterized some of the Haight–Ashbury thinking of the sixties. We are moving, I believe, toward a generation which is prepared to do some hard thinking about both means and ends. And we can all take heart that this is the path our young people are choosing.

Newsletter, *May 29, 1975*

Freedom of the Press

"Congress shall make no law . . . abridging the freedom . . . of the press . . ." So states the First Amendment to our Constitution. Was this because the writers recognized an important abstract principle, a necessary safeguard for the citizen against possible wrongdoing by government itself? Or was it perhaps the simple expression of a desire to protect what had been for them a very handy weapon against a government they regarded as despotic? In other words, was it principle or pragmatism?

My own view is that it was—and is—both. The revolutionary "broadsides" that could be written and distributed by any citizen–printer were powerful in their public effect. They were useful in the Revolution, just as the publication of governmental scandals today is useful as punishment and deterrent. But I think there is something more and this is being brought into sharp focus by the actions of the United Nations Educational, Scientific, and Cultural Organization—UNESCO.

The principle that UNESCO is endangering, and that the First Amendment establishes, is that the press belongs to the people, and that no government, even one elected by the people, can limit or censor it. All democratic societies which depend on the consent of the governed recognize this to a greater or lesser degree. In the dictatorships, on the other hand—whether left or right—the press is regarded as the instrument of the state, a way to increase the power of those who hold power, a way to manipulate and control the people.

Consider this press law of October 4, 1933, directing editors "to keep out of newspapers anything which in any manner . . . tends to weaken the strength of the German Reich, outwardly or inwardly . . . or offends the honor and dignity of Germany."

It was Hitler's government which published this, but it is gospel in many countries of the Socialist camp today.

It is also, regrettably, allied in spirit to a growing trend in UNESCO, which set up the MacBride Commission to study the complaints of Third World countries. They felt that their news and views were inadequately reported in the world press, and in many ways this seemed a valid complaint. They obviously did not have the means of disseminating information as compared to the industrialized countries. Had the commission stopped with recommendations for helping them with equipment and technology, no harm would have been done.

But the commission's report, and subsequent UNESCO meetings, did not stop there. They went on from *means* to *content,* from helping disadvantaged nations to an obvious effort to control the press of the free world. One report, for example, outlined a code for journalists, and suggested that they be licensed (with the implication that licenses could be revoked for violation of the code). It proposed also "the right of reply," which means that any government could demand equal space—or time—for rebuttal of a report found offensive.

Our U.S. officials have protested to no avail. The answer has always been that these are only proposals, that the MacBride report is "a study." But the trend is unmistakable, culminating in an official UNESCO meeting early this year to which no Western journalists were invited.

Luckily, these journalists objected vigorously, demanded admittance to the meeting—as was their right—and finally organized an unofficial meeting of their own. This took place at Talloires in France, where the UNESCO Director-General had to hear the unvarnished Western view. To back up our official U.S. members of UNESCO, Representative Bob Shamansky (Democrat from Ohio) and I have introduced a resolution on the subject. Ambassador Kirkpatrick, our ambassador to the UN itself, is well aware of the danger and is vigilant.

Perhaps it is not surprising that there should be this controversy about communications. Many have said that the "communications revolution" of this century ranks in importance with the industrial revolution as an element in social change. Certainly it is true that we have mastered its technology without fully understanding its psychological implications. An increasing number of governments seems to fear the power of a free press. Mexico, for example, has just issued press regulations that outlaw publication of materials which "directly or indirectly degrade or rebuff the Mexican people, their abilities, customs, and traditions . . ." Heavy fines and penalties await violators of the rules. And Mexico is not alone.

The first hint I ever had of this regrettable development was at a meeting of the nations which had signed the Helsinki Final Act. The Soviet bloc wanted every signatory government to discourage any critical reporting about other signatory countries. The immediate reaction of the representative of the Netherlands showed the gulf between East and West.

"We have fifty-two newspapers in my country," he said, "each expressing a different point of view, so the citizen can choose. If I agreed to such a proposal, my countrymen would think me mad."

There was a stunned silence. His was the voice of the West, speaking not backed by the power of huge armies or of nuclear arms but by the power of an idea. The subject was dropped.

I believe it is true that, however practical the motives of those who wrote it, the First Amendment embodies a principle that is central to Western civilization. We had better cherish it.

Newsletter, *August 26, 1981*

An Independent Judiciary

I was horrified, as a Republican ashamed, that Mr. Nixon had appointed 92 percent of his 45 judges as Republican. Mr. Carter noticed it and in his campaign he said, "This has got to stop. The appointment of U.S. Attorneys and federal judges must be non-political." But Mr. Carter's judicial appointments were 96 percent Democratic the last time I asked, worse than Mr. Nixon's. And he had not just 45, but more than 200, because the Democratic Congress wouldn't vote the money for the extra federal judgeships when they hoped to get a Democrat as president. So they held up on that and the courts were jammed, and they got it—they got just what they wanted, a whole bunch of political appointments.

The system is so bad that when the list of six new judges for New Jersey was first proposed, I was horrified to see one or two of those names. I went to the head of our delegation, also chairman of our Judiciary Committee here in the House, Peter Rodino, a man for whom I have high regard. He handled the Nixon proceedings with such reverence for the Constitution that it was a model. I went to him and I said, "I can't stand this. This is a disgrace to the state. We're going to be the laughing stock of the press. We cannot have this. I don't want to do anything behind your back. You are the dean of our delegation and the chairman of the Judiciary Committee. I want you to know what I'm doing. I'm going to Attorney General Bell and I'm going to tell him that if this goes through, I'm going to have to protest in the press."

He didn't say "Don't." He didn't say anything very much. He did say a few things but perhaps he wouldn't want to be quoted. Anyway, he knew the names as well as I did, and the objections. And so, he didn't try to stop me.

I went to see Attorney General Bell at eight o'clock in the morning, and I had armed myself with a list which I got from the administrative officer of the courts, Mr. Simpson. I listed his full name, address and telephone number, his opinion of the various women judges in the state of New Jersey. Two "giants" were starred. (He said, "Those two are really giants and would grace any court, but these six are fine women judges too.")

I got all the names and the courts that they presided over, and asked, "Would you mind giving me their political affiliations if you can?" All but one were Democrats. So the Attorney General wouldn't be embarrassed.

All this was written down carefully, and off I went to breakfast, and I told the Attorney General the source of my information and why I was so upset. Most of my information came from the press, so therefore I couldn't prove anything. I had no information of my own knowledge, except what reporter friends had told me. I gave him the opinion of Mr. Simpson, and I told Mr. Bell in no uncertain terms that if these appointments went through as planned, I would feel compelled to go to the press. There's a point where you have to draw the line. I don't know what the public thinks, but when you read in the paper that a federal judge has been appointed for the district covering Arkansas, Wyoming, or whatever, and that he was the campaign manager of the successful Republican or Democratic senator, how does it look? How does it look to the public? What do they say? "Same old game. Forget the promise to keep the courts clean." Surely our judicial system, like the Constitution and the free press, is one of the essential strengths that keep our people free.

_____

Taped interview, January 15, 1981

Academic Freedom

A new Federal agency—a Department of Education separate from the Department of Health, Education and Welfare —has been planned for some time. And for a long time I was in favor of it. I spoke and wrote supporting the idea. But now a longer experience in Washington is beginning to erode my confidence in the belief that we could keep a relatively free educational system under a federal department solely devoted to that subject, or that we could establish a whole new bureaucracy without incurring extra costs.

Here is an example which shows what is already happening to education in America. In western Pennsylvania there is a small college affiliated with the United Presbyterian Church. It is called Grove City College and has 2,200 students with a faculty of 110. It has never sought or received any federal money for research, development, or anything else. It has low tuition and no indebtedness.

Two years ago, however, a letter beginning "Dear Recipient" arrived from HEW, ordering the college to complete forms showing compliance with Title IX of the Education Act. This title is concerned with sex discrimination and this was the college's position on that issue as stated by the college president, Charles McKenzie: "Grove City doesn't have any quarrel with the intent of the Title IX regulations. As a matter of Christian belief, it has treated males and females equitably long before HEW was created." Further, the college was not a "recipient," so the letter was ignored. An exchange followed. HEW threatened to cut off student aid: "I was told in strong terms," said the college president, "that they would bring us 'into compliance one way or another.' " The case came before the courts. HEW admitted that the college receives no funds but held that aid to the students in the form of grants and guaranteed loans constitutes indirect benefit to the college, even though none of the aid is granted to or through the college itself, which only certifies as to student attendance.

The administrative law judge ruled, in effect, in favor of HEW, upholding the right of HEW to cut off student funds. The college and four of its students have appealed to the Federal District Court in Pittsburgh, with a complaint against HEW. And there the matter now rests. HEW has not cut off funds to the students, but meanwhile both sides are put to considerable expense to resolve the issue—the public paying for one side, the college for the other, and the public interest hanging in the balance.

Some comments on this case are interesting. The administrative judge: "There was not the slightest hint of any failure to comply with Title IX, save the refusal to submit an executed assurance of compliance. . . . This refusal is obviously a matter of conscience and belief."

The president of the college: "This issue is one of jurisdiction. As we do not accept any state or federal funds, we do not believe HEW has any jurisdiction over the college. We reject the philosophy that government should fund or control the private sector of American society. Our stand is one on the principle of independence and freedom."

The controversy is not as simple as it might seem. At first glance, the action of HEW can be condemned as heavy-handed, unfair, and unwarranted. But there is an inescapable duty on the part of all government agencies to see to it that the tax monies of the public are spent in support of, never in defiance of, the law. This may, and often does, mean that the agency must have the power to compel obedience. The weakness of the government's case in this particular instance is that the method used to compel compliance was to hurt a third party—the students. It is to be hoped that the federal judge will rule for the college, because the law, as written, applies only to institutions accepting federal money, and, not incidentally, as the college is apparently absolutely fair to the female students. But the importance of the case goes beyond the immediate example.

If there's one thing one learns in Washington, it is that all agencies—without any exception that I have been able to discover—strive for more and more control over whatever section of society is under their jurisdiction. Power has its charms for everyone. The men who wrote the Constitution knew it and tried to frustrate an uninterrupted flow of power, weakening it by dividing it into different channels.

To concentrate a new federal agency on education seems to me now a dangerous step. The freedom and diversity of our system is traditional and most valuable. We need the splendid mix of schools, colleges, and universities, both public and private. It is argued that almost every nation has a separate Department of Education, but it is not always mentioned that in France, for example, the same textbook is, we are proudly told, being expounded in every specified grade, at the same hour, on the same day, in every school in the country. To us, this would be anathema, totally contrary to the system we have admired.

We already have, perhaps, too many federal agencies, grown to a size that was never even imagined when the Constitution was written, so the task of limiting their power evolves upon us. It is a job that needs doing every day and the concerned citizen, who cares enough to protest, is the best source of constructive action.

Newsletter, *June 14, 1979*

Small Business and Big Government

As a member of the Small Business and Banking Committees, I have had a number of surprises which may be as interesting to you as they were to me.

Item: A small businessman, anxious to comply with the new regulations of the Federal Reserve Board, wrote the Federal Trade Commission (FTC), which is charged by the Federal Reserve Board with implementation of regulations. He asked if the contract he was offering his customers was in compliance and the answer was yes.

However, when a class-action suit was brought against him he found that the FTC letter of approval contained a caveat that it was "advisory only." A big business could have afforded a corporation counsel who might have caught the implication, but the small businessman could not, and he was ruined. I proposed an amendment to correct this and the whole bill has already passed the House. But it seems absurd that we have developed a system which allows a formally established arm of the government, charged with implementing regulations, to dodge responsibility for the advice it gives a citizen who simply wants to do the right thing.

Item: A small businessman, hoping to set up a chartered bus service from New Jersey to Florida, was told that the field was already served by two companies and that he could not get a license from the Interstate Commerce Commission (ICC). The President's proposals for some "deregulation"—some changes in the regulations and policies of the ICC—are a step in correcting this obvious curtailment of individual enterprise and freedom, and I am working with several fellow members of Congress to move in that direction.

Item: A number of companies (airlines and trucking companies, for example) have regulated rates under the Federal Aviation Agency (FAA) and the ICC. No lower rates are allowed and the punishment for violations is heavy. If these rates were not approved by these agencies, the companies involved would be subject to immediate antitrust action, especially since, in some cases, it is the companies themselves which agree on a certain rate, and the agency which approves it. Certainly, we must ask if this system is in the public interest.

Item: A small businessman explained to our Committee the effect the paperwork the government requires has had on his company:

> Consider these frightening figures. In the past eleven months, our small company was required to read, compile, study, fill out 438 Government forms totaling 2,267 pages.
>
> This paper mountain made it necessary for us to move into larger headquarters to find additional storage space just to file our copies of these records. We were required to hire another bookkeeper and still farm out some of the more sophisticated forms to a national accounting firm, Ernst & Ernst. Think of it, two bookkeepers in an office staff of only six people. But, while we may have been able to hire Ernst & Ernst, think of the burden on the small shopkeeper in Clive or Oskaloosa, Iowa. What does he do about it?
>
> We estimate our costs for shuffling all this paper at $19,000, almost equal to our annual net profit average for five years."

This short list of items is only partial, of course. We have been working on a number of other cases, such as those involving small businesses caught in contracts with the federal government, when a change in government policy changes basic costs and threatens to wipe out a small business entirely. (I have co-sponsored legislation which corrects this and it has been signed by the President.) But the list shows that government can and does harm, or at best hamper, free enterprise and competition. In many cases, the public—the consumer—all unaware, is paying the cost. A system which permits all this is especially hard on small business, which is the backbone of our economy. Small business employs forty-six million of the seventy-one million workers in private employment in this country, or 53 percent if one includes the fifteen million in federal, state, county, and municipal government. The definition of a small business varies with each industry—a small steel manufacturer, for example, would necessarily employ far more people than a small dress manufacturer. But the National Small Business Association estimates that there are 21,200,000 people employed in companies with fewer than fifty employees; of the nearly thirteen million firms in the United States over half have fewer than three employees.

The need to protect the public, to protect the worker, to ensure that each pays his fair share—all these are the reasons for the proliferation of paperwork and they are basically good reasons. However, this paperwork is costing the companies about eighteen billion a year, according to the statisticians of the AFL–CIO. The cost to the taxpayers of hiring the government workers who must read and analyze the reports is another heavy burden. If not controlled, this paperwork could strangle us, much as was the Byzantine Empire, in a noose of red tape.

Newsletter, *February 5, 1976*

Even-Steven

I am sure this resolution is wise, but I wish it were accompanied by another addressed to the manufacturers of this country.

Why is there this trade imbalance? It is because the Japanese products are satisfactory to the people of this country.

I received a letter this morning from a constituent which explains so well what is happening. All her life this woman and her family have purchased American products, specifically cars of one particular manufacturer. On this American automobile, the muffler was gone and had to be replaced twice. The brackets fell out. The fan broke. Everything happened in just one year and one month, so the warranty did not hold.

I regret to say, she now has a three-year-old Japanese car that has never had the slightest trouble of any kind. The dealer calls up to remind her, "You know it is time you had servicing again." And the warranty is for five years.

Until we make cars, and everything else which the American people want to buy, our market is going to be invaded.

I do agree that there needs to be a warning to the Japanese government, that we believe in free trade, but it has to be fair.

If their tariffs are raised against us, our tariffs should be raised against them in a reciprocal mood, even-steven. We should be firm that if they keep our products out, we will retaliate. This is not because we are becoming protectionists; this is because we are insisting on even-steven, fair trade and free trade.

However, Mr. Speaker, we should warn our manufacturers.

We cannot go on like this. Our consumers would suffer if we did put enormous tariffs on the things they want to buy. That is not the way.

The way is competition. The way is excellence. The way is quality in our products. I think we ought to send a resolution of this kind to our manufacturers.

Debate on Resolution calling upon Japan to reduce
trade imbalance with U.S.
Congressional Record, *November 17, 1980*

A Case Against Government Subsidy

A most disappointing thing has come to light—a large campaign gift from a group of special-interests, followed by a measure for which the public will have to pay. The measure is the proposed Cargo Preference bill, which would require that the percentage of oil brought into the United States by U.S.-flag vessels must rise every year from 3.5 percent, which it is now, to 9.5 percent by October 1982. The cost to consumers will be high.

We all remember an earlier example of this—$100,000 to President Nixon, $50,000 each to Senator McGovern, Senator Humphrey, and Representative Wilbur Mills, given by the dairy interests and followed by a rise in the support price of milk.

The sad thing is that, according to *Common Cause,* "over $100,000 in maritime industry contributions" were given to President Carter and are now being followed by his support for this bill. *The New York Times,* in its analysis of Comptroller General Staats' latest report to the House Merchant Marine and Fisheries Committee, estimates "the cost to the consumer of the cargo preference bill at between $550 million and $610 million a year."

Who will pay these costs? Consumers will pay in home heating bills, gasoline prices, utility bills, and higher costs (which will be passed on to consumers) for every industry which uses oil.

Who wants such a bill? Not the Department of Defense, although defense requirements are often used to excuse the

$786 million the maritime interests already get every year from the Treasury, and although the department has testified that it does not need tankers—the only ships involved in the bill. Not the State Department, which must be worried about the treaties we have with over 30 countries, which would be violated by the proposed bill. Not the Council of Economic Advisers, "which estimates the net impact on the economy as a whole would be a decrease in total employment and Gross National Product," nor the Economic Policy Group (EPG), as its chairman, Treasury Secretary Blumenthal, wrote in a memorandum to the President included in the committee report. "In March, the EPG unanimously recommended that you oppose oil cargo preference legislation, and suggested we might explore alternative ways of assisting the maritime industry."

Who wants such a bill? The answer is the maritime interests and unfortunately, the Committee on Merchant Marine and Fisheries. According to a CBS *60 Minutes* program last October, 30 of the 39 members of the committee received contributions from these special interests. And now, by a vote of 31 to 5, the bill has been favorably reported by the committee and will come to the House for action. Only the press and the public can save us now.

Newsletter, *September 22, 1977*

What do we do for the maritime interests now? According to the *Wall Street Journal,* the tax-subsidized wages of the average U.S. seaman are $24,000 a year and the marine engineers, of course, "do considerably better."

For the shipowners, the *Wall Street Journal* reports, "The Federation of American Controlled Shipping estimates that the crude carrier *Stuyvesant,* just completed in the Brooklyn Seatrain shipyard and chartered to Sohio, will gross $30 million in three years on a $9-million equity investment. The government paid a $27-million subsidy on the $63-million ship and also insured a mortgage for the sums borrowed to build it. Not a bad deal."

Yes, indeed. It is more than a sad thing—it is an outrage.

The facts are these. The Merchant Marine was costing $746 million a year in 1977. What does that go for? It goes to pay about three quarters, 70 percent, 72 percent, of the Merchant Marine wages. Taxpayers are paying this because our Merchant Marine seaman gets $24,000 a year, each one, and we pay something like $12 thousand out of the $20 thousand dollars. We pay about 50 percent of the construction of every ship. The S.S. *Stuyvesant* went down the ways in Brooklyn, and it cost $60 million. The company puts up something like $15 million and the government, we the taxpayers, put up something like $28 million. It's really shocking.

Now, it's all done under the guise of defense. "We have to have a Merchant Marine," they say, "in case of war." Very well. Let the Defense Department tell us what they need. Let the Defense Department tell us how many ships of what kind and size are required on a standby basis for defense reasons.

The folly of the Cargo Preference bill was that you couldn't possibly justify it on the basis of defense, because defense doesn't need that many tankers. That's not the way things are done. And in any case, the Defense Department said they had enough tankers, and didn't want any more.

The money was for the Merchant Marine and the shipping interests. The unions and the companies wanted it, and they both pay enormous sums in campaign contributions. Is it possible we're going to go on like this?

So I wrote a newsletter about it. The last words were, "Only the press and the public can save us now." And the press saved us. There were editorials from Bangor to Los Angeles.

And when it came to the crunch here in the House, people didn't dare vote for it, because it had become so notorious.

That's the best example I know of the press stepping in and saving the public from enormous useless expenses. Nothing to justify it in the way of defense or anything else. You wonder sometimes how these people get reelected. It seems so nakedly obvious.

Taped interview, February 4, 1980

To the Editor:

David Fairbank White made some excellent points in his October 6 Op–Ed article on the state of the U.S. maritime industry ("Reforging U.S. Hulls"), but I must disagree with some of his conclusions.

Mr. White favors continuing the flow of government subsidies to the industry, despite their obvious failure to maintain the health of the industry. The taxpayers have spent over $2.2 billion on direct construction and operating subsidies in the last four years alone. In fiscal year 1982, they will spend another $417 million on operating subsidies, of which $354.6 million is for wage subsidies alone. This works out to a cost of $61,282 for each of the 5,786 billets on subsidized ships.

Mr. White also refers to the need for "a fuller consideration" of cargo preference programs, which require that a given percentage of government-financed cargoes be shipped on U.S.-flag vessels. Simply stated, these are hidden subsidies which do not show up in the budget of the Maritime Administration but which, when combined with direct maritime subsidies, bring the total amount that taxpayers contribute to the maritime programs to well over $2 billion a year.

One of the main effects of cargo preference requirements on our Title I "Food for Peace" program, for example, is to keep inefficient, unsafe, and generally ancient ships at sea. This fact was brought to the public's attention last October by the sinking of the U.S.S. *Poet,* which took the lives of 34 American seamen. The *Poet,* an aging ship, bound for Egypt with U.S. government food aid, had a history of safety problems and was too old and inefficient to operate profitably in commercial shipping.

The subsidies are justified on the basis of national defense, although as the fate of the *Poet* demonstrates, many of the creaking old vessels being kept alive by cargo preference would be of no military value during a national security emergency. In fact, more than half of the bulk fleet which carries P.L.-480 Title I food aid was built before 1949.

What the U.S. maritime industry *does* need is less government involvement, fewer costly federal regulations, and a reduction in the unnecessary costs which impair the U.S. fleet's ability to compete successfully. It is worth noting, for example, that the Maritime Administration recently approved a manning level of 34 for a new class of diesel-powered vessels, while Sweden has agreed with its unions to man the same type of ships with a crew of 17.

Equally noteworthy is the fact that, despite the existence of construction subsidies which pay 50 percent of the cost of building in the United States, many companies opt to build their ships abroad because building in the United States costs two and a half to three times as much. Interestingly, the most profitable American shipping company, and the world's largest containership line, receives no government construction or operating subsidies, yet it consistently outperforms the industry.

The New York Times, *October 13, 1981*

Deregulate Trucking

There are all sorts of macroeconomic ideas about inflation —its causes and cures. This report deals with a small, simple, practical idea. It is no panacea, but it is something which could be done right now to lower the cost of food: We could exempt all food from the regulations of the Interstate Commerce Commission (ICC).

At the moment, and for many years since the ICC started regulating trucking, fresh agricultural produce has been almost entirely exempt from regulation. In other words, independent truckers who hold no franchise or permit from the ICC can carry fresh produce any place, any time, for any farmer. (There are certain curious exceptions to this—bananas, for example, are not exempt—but by and large, fresh produce is.)

The belief that exemption would lower the cost of food is based on the story of what happened to chickens. In 1956, the Supreme Court of the United States upheld a district court decision that fresh, plucked, eviscerated chickens were no longer to be subject to regulation by the ICC. The cost of distributing those chickens dropped by 33 percent. This figure can be found in speeches by Lewis Engman, former head of the Federal Trade Commission, and in other more recent speeches, notably an address by the Assistant Attorney General of the Antitrust Division, John H. Shenefield, in February of this year. He remarked that in the mid-fifties "fresh and frozen poultry and frozen fruits and vegetables were changed from regulated to exempt commodities. Rates dropped thirty-three percent on poultry and nineteen percent on fruits and vegetables . . ."

The argument that is often used against deregulation of trucking is that little towns and hamlets would be bereft of deliveries. But what hamlet is bereft of milk and eggs now? As Assistant Attorney General Shenefield said, when the exemptions were granted, ". . . service actually improved."

This is no giant step against inflation, but it does strike at the cost of the most basic essential—food. When one considers that the wheat in a 38-cent loaf of bread costs only three and a half cents, any part of the difference should be a matter for study and concern. Everything connected with trucking—gasoline, drivers' wages, insurance, auto repairs, interest rates on the loan that bought the truck—are all far higher than they were twenty years ago; so the proportion of savings may well be much more. It is hard to imagine exactly what the effect on home budgets might be if all food—canned food, butchered meat, everything—were exempted from regulation.

If we wanted to strike another blow against inflation we could exempt fuel oil for home heating from the provisions of the Jones Act. This act, requiring that all goods shipped between American ports must be carried in American ships, adds *by itself* 90 cents to every barrel of oil coming up from Gulf refineries—90 cents more than if the oil came from the Bahamas. I have introduced a bill on the food problem and it may well pass—a number of my colleagues have expressed interest in it. The fuel-oil bill will be more difficult because shipping interests will oppose it. But, like food, home heating is a basic necessity and certainly this is the time for any help the public can get.

Newsletter, *May 17, 1979*

Mr. Speaker, in the past few days many people have called my office with questions concerning my effort to amend H.R. 6418, the Motor Carrier Act of 1980, to exempt all food products from Interstate Commerce Commission (ICC) regulation. Here, then, are a few of the most commonly asked questions and their answers:

1. What exactly would your amendment do?

My amendment would add a new section to Paragraph 10526 of the Interstate Commerce Act—"Miscellaneous motor carrier transportation exemptions." Products already exempt under this section include ordinary livestock, a variety of unprocessed food items, i.e., fresh vegetables and plucked chickens, and shellfish. Vehicles already exempt under this section include newspaper delivery trucks, farm vehicles, school buses, and taxicabs. My amendment would exempt any "food and other edible product (including edible byproducts but excluding alcoholic beverages and drugs) intended for human consumption." It does not include pet food or any other grocery items not intended for human consumption.

2. Would the Fenwick amendment benefit consumers?

Yes. The amendment would increase conpetition in the trucking industry—always a healthy sign for consumers. But even more the amendment would specifically cut certain costs of transporting the items to be deregulated. My amendment would help balance traffic flows and thus save fuel costs. For instance, today a trucker carrying tomatoes from Maryland to New Jersey for processing into soup cannot then pick up a load of soup. With passage of my amendment he/she could.

A recent survey of poultry shippers rated unregulated carrier service better than regulated service 95 percent of the time. Support from such groups as Common Cause, Congress Watch, and Consumers' Union, as well as almost every agricultural group, shows widespread consumer support for my amendment.

Inflation is the greatest enemy of those citizens who are on fixed incomes but there are many thousands more who are merely trying to keep their heads above water. Food is the largest item in a family's budget and anything we could do to help out would be most welcome. Transportation accounts for 5.2 cents out of every food dollar spent. If this amendment succeeds we would be able to save consumers anywhere from 13 cents to $1.30 on every $50 purchase of groceries. It is a simple first step in the fight against inflation.

3. Didn't the Senate take action on a similar proposal when they considered their version of trucking deregulation?

Yes, the Senate Commerce Committee adopted a virtually identical amendment to S. 2245. An effort to delete this amendment was defeated on the Senate floor by a vote of 39 to 47. Thus, approval of my amendment would concur with the action already taken by the Senate.

4. Wouldn't small towns suffer if the Fenwick amendment is adopted and all food products are exempted?

No. The bulk of small community service is currently provided by non-regulated motor carriers. Furthermore, unprocessed foods are presently exempt from ICC regulation. What small town is bereft of fresh fruits and vegetables? A Department of Transportation study released last November characterized the service to small towns in Nevada, Kentucky, and New Mexico as "adequate" largely because of the service provided by unregulated intrastate private carriers. The service provided by regulated carriers, the same study revealed, was "infrequent, slow, and often at rates which were perceived as high." I think the evidence is abundant and clear that deregulating all food products would not adversely affect small communities.

5. I've heard some independent owner-operators complain that adoption of the Fenwick amendment would eliminate the 13 percent fuel surcharge mandated by the ICC. Is this true and how will your amendment aid these small businessmen of the trucking industry?

When hauling items exempted under my amendment the benefits of the fuel surcharge would be lost. But the loss would be more than made up for by the ability of the independents to compete in previously regulated commodities. The fuel surcharge is a 13 percent passthrough from the shipper to the independent based on the ICC-set tariff. Independents, after passage of my amendment, would be able to haul all food products without "trip-leasing" to a regulated carrier. A trip-lease involves paying the owner of ICC authority—in this case the regulated carrier—anywhere from 25 percent to 40 percent of the tariff for the right to haul regulated goods under the aegis of the authority. Some carriers do not own a single truck but prosper by using independents exclusively. After passage of my amendment the independents could carry any food items without paying a regulated carrier what is, in effect, monopoly rent. Because the regulated carrier would not be skimming 25 to 40 percent off the shipper's payment for services, the independent would, in my opinion and the opinion of experts in the field, benefit financially with passage of my amendment.

6. What about the charge that chaos already exists in the exempt trucking industry?

Not true. A recent study done by the University of Pennsylvania for the Department of Transportation found that the intrastate trucking industry in New Jersey—which is unregulated—was stable and highly competitive. Rates in this market were, on average, 15 percent lower than rates for similar transportation in the regulated interstate market. The study also found, again, that unregulated service was equal to or better than service provided by regulated carriers and is more profitable for the unregulated carrier. A majority of shippers and carriers prefer the lack of regulation within New Jersey.

7. Won't expansion of the agricultural exemption result in decreased safety?

No. Safety provisions for the motor carrier industry are under the purview of the Department of Transportation and are unaffected by the status of ICC regulation or lack of regulation. The exempt industry currently has the same safety standards as the regulated industry and this will continue with the passage of H.R. 6418. In addition, H.R. 6418 includes minimum insurance coverage for operators as part of the fit, willing, and able requirement. This section of the bill is administered by the Secretary of Transportation and provides for financial responsibility of $1 million for carriers —whether regulated or exempt—engaged in interstate commerce. I might also point out that an individual with a rather large investment in trucking equipment is more likely to preserve his equipment in safe condition than a trucking firm which owns a number of trucks and the driver does not possess pride of ownership.

A footnote: The amendment failed in the House, thanks mostly to opponents who claimed that "a delicate balance" had been achieved in the bill. When asked for a translation of "a delicate balance," the answer was, "They struck a deal."

Congressional Record, *June 3, 1980*

Regulation with a Human Face

Some of the regulations which govern so much of our lives cry out for a waiver system: a well-defined process for making exceptions to the rule when the rule is crushing the very people it was designed to protect. Here are three examples:

Nursing Homes. A 94-year-old woman is happy in a nursing home which costs $210 a week. After two and a half years there, paying her way, she has run out of funds and is eligible for tax support. The nursing home has many advantages: She loves it; it is approved by state and local authorities; and her 74-year-old son lives within five miles and can visit almost daily. But the nursing home does not meet the staffing requirements of the responsible federal agency—Health and Human Services. The nursing homes in the area are full so the old lady may be sent to a home far away, at a cost to the taxpayers of $350 per week. The family is desperate, and it seems a clear case of regulatory overkill—unnecessary suffering for the old lady and her family, unnecessary expense for the taxpayers.

But, as in both the other cases that will be cited here, more careful study shows the need for regulations. Scandals have revealed the fact that the taxpayers' money has occasionally been used to enrich a nursing home owner at the expense of the patients. Only clearly established standards can prevent this, and yet it does seem outrageous that a benevolent and prudent intention can cause so much hardship to all concerned. The answer, I believe, is a waiver which should be requested by the Regional Director of Health and Human Services, the State Director of Licensing and Certification, and the local health authorities—state and county.

CETA. The Comprehensive Education and Training Act has given rise to a good deal of controversy. In fact, in one New Jersey county the local administrators have been sued by the NAACP. Most of the trouble arises through sections IId and VI, where employment training for public service jobs is provided for. Section VII however, is less controversial. It trains for private sector employment and here there are two compelling regulations: 1. the trainees cannot replace workers who would otherwise be employed; and 2. nothing the trainees produce can result in profit to the employer. Both are needed to protect other employers from one who could otherwise, in agreement with a lax administrator, undercut any competitor by using these federal funds.

But the Fifth District lost an excellent training program when the company's counsel read the second of these two regulations. About 20 young unemployed trainees were to have been taught the skills needed for regular work in a fine company, but it was impossible to promise that some of the items these trainees produced might not pass inspection and enter the regular product line. The company withdrew, and so did two other companies which had been planning similar programs. The Business Council, the local AFL–CIO Council, the local CETA administrator, and the Regional Administrator for the Federal Department of Labor should have been able to request and obtain a waiver from Washington as soon as the company's counsel raised the issue. But no such waiver process was in place and the whole constructive endeavor was lost.

H.U.D. The Federal Department of Housing and Urban Development has had to set up certain regulations when federal funds are being used to supplement the rent payments an indigent person can afford to make. The standards contain certain specific requirements, including—in the case that came to my attention—a bathroom sink. It seems sensible. One cannot approve using public funds—the taxpayers' money—to give landlords infinite scope for renting substandard housing. But consider this case: An indigent woman, frightened from her apartment by a burglar, found another, perfect for her, with a resident manager and a pay phone in the corridor just outside her door. But the bathroom had no sink so the rent subsidy was in question. The fact that the woman had a back injury and never used any sink lower than a kitchen sink did not seem to matter. After too many calls and letters and too much effort, the situation was finally resolved, but only because a rudimentary waiver system is provided by HUD. The system conspicuously lacks, however, the clear procedure which would resolve such problems quickly and easily.

These three cases all come from real life. Except the CETA project, which failed, the dilemmas were finally solved in a sensible way, but only after an enormous expenditure of time and effort. When one considers the huge appropriations for these programs it is heartbreaking when, as is too often the case, the regulations and requirements do not allow for consideration of the suffering and special needs of the people who supposedly should benefit. The fact that savings—rather than extra expenditure—are usually the result is certainly another valid reason for change. The obvious conclusion is that we must try to persuade the various departments to agree to a waiver system and that is what I plan to do.

Newsletter, *February 25, 1981*

Start with a Person

Mr. Chairman, if we do not force these agencies to work together, instead of separating people into categories we will continue to spend money in the useless duplication of services. Congress must insist that they do so.

In my district, for example, if you are an elderly person with 3(B) transportation, you have difficulty getting into title XX buses, although both are for old people. What we ought to do is build the program from the person, not from the agency and from the title. And everybody ought to be able to use the section 8 housing restaurant so that we do not have to set up a whole separate program for people who may live across the street. Unless we can somehow begin to get common sense into the operation of these programs, our old people are going to suffer and our taxpayers also.

Debate on funding program for the elderly
Congressional Record, *July 24, 1980*

Health

Health care services need complete reorganization and streamlining. The general public, reading reports of the various plans proposed by the various political figures, may well believe that there is nothing now available beyond Blue Cross–Blue Shield and whatever the private insurance companies have to offer.

The truth is that enormous sums are already being expended by the Federal and State governments, while the average family cowers under the threat of a catastrophic illness.

Hospital care, whether paid by Medicare or Medicaid funds, now costs $175 to $200 a day and nursing home care in New Jersey averages $45 to $50 a day. Many patients are kept in hospitals longer than necessary because, particularly in New Jersey, there is a shortage of nursing home beds. And many patients are in nursing homes who do not need skilled care and would be much happier at home, with some health care, which costs about $18 to $23 a visit. The estimate of the number of such people in New Jersey is 3,000.

This looks like a logjam that could easily be remedied by more home health care, resulting in more open nursing home beds, and fewer people kept in the hospital longer than necessary. But no problem is that simple. Although an income of $624 a month will not disqualify a patient for nursing home care, no one whose income is over $208 per month can, in New Jersey, be given publicly-funded home health care. Nor can hospitals move patients who need only skilled nursing care, or intermediate care, into empty hospital wards with support from federal funding, because the federal regulations require that hospitals charge *costs* per bed. I have suggested a simple change in the regulations: ". . . at cost *or less";* and, more complicated, I have also suggested a tax-free stipend of half the cost of nursing home care to be given those who qualify for nursing home care but need nothing more than home health care. What we have now is a patchwork of programs and, in a way, these suggestions would add to the quilt. What is obviously needed is a whole revision and consolidation of the various programs.

As long as states set the income level for one program and the federal government has another set of criteria for the others, with some programs fully federally funded and others shared between state and federal, there is bound to be trouble. Many who have studied the problem believe that all Medical programs, including those for the disabled, should be consolidated into one, and removed from Social Security entirely. Social Security would then be a pension plan only. Many others, while not disagreeing with this view, are convinced that all programs for the elderly, at least, should be under one new heading, Title XXI of the Social Security Act, eliminating Title XVIII (Medicare), Title XIX (Medicaid), Title XX (Social Services) and Title III (Older Americans Act). This would remove income eligibility disparities and consolidate funding.

The hope for substantive structural changes in the whole health services field is dimmed by the fact that a number of different Committees of Congress have some jurisdiction. Social Security legislation goes to Ways and Means; Social Services to the Committee on Interstate and Foreign Commerce, and also to the Committee on Education and Labor. (The Select Committee on the Aging makes recommendations on legislation affecting the elderly, but has no legislative powers.) And, meanwhile, as one Morris County social worker told me, and as reported in one of my newsletters, an elderly person eligible for aid under one Title may have to watch a half-empty bus go by, because it is only for those eligible under another Title. I am working continually with Chairman Pepper and Representative Grassley (Ranking Minority Member) of the Select Committee on the Aging, to try and find a way to solve these problems; I am cosponsor of other measures, including the Medicaid Community Care Act of 1980 which will at least allow patients who now meet the Medicaid income standards for nursing home eligibility to have the option of receiving home health care. This would help the situation by giving the patient a choice and saving the taxpayers' money, but the tangle of jurisdictions and funding will only be solved by a complete, structural reordering.

Newsletter, *April 2, 1980*

Urban Experiments

Why are cities in trouble? There is no need to list the troubles—they are well known. The answer to the question of the cause has been that the middle class and the affluent are moving out, taking their tax-paying ability with them, while the poor move in, driven from the farms, where machinery has replaced them, needing more and increasingly expensive services.

We have seen this as a peculiarly American problem, but it isn't. The hearings of the City Subcommittee of the Banking, Finance and Urban Affairs Committee have been an eye-opening experience. We have heard urban experts and planners from Germany, Britain, Sweden, Denmark, and the Netherlands. Cities everywhere are coming up against the same problems.

After the Second World War, and into the 1960s, cities grew alarmingly. The displaced were streaming out of the countryside, the shanty towns and crowded slums were expanding. But then the tide reversed itself. In the 1970s, the exodus from the cities began.

Sometimes this reversal came about through deliberate action by a central government. "New towns" and "satellite towns" were set up, with carefully planned transportation, housing, and employment opportunities. This was done most notably in Sweden and Britain. But in many cases, the effect was unexpected. The middle class and the skilled workers moved willingly to the new towns, leaving the unskilled and the most depressed in the central cities.

In Holland, as the Dutch official told us, affluence made it possible for people to move out of the central city. And the inevitable result for the city is the common, apparently worldwide experience in developed countries: parking problems, traffic congestion, air polluted by the automobiles of commuters, a diminished tax base, and greater need for services for those left behind.

Transportation plans were on every expert's tongue. Obviously, if every Briton who can afford what they call "a second home" is leaving town—if every Muscovite must have a dacha—mass transport is the first thought. But even here there was a surprise: "Declining patronage of transportation systems" was reported by one planner.

In a way, the hearings have been disappointing in the sense that every avenue seemed to close the farther one traveled down it. Many of the mayors of American towns testified that federal takeover of welfare would solve the problem, as though there was no heartache in our cities but the financial concerns of the governing officials.

The most important problem is that of the people involved. What kind of life will they have? We must know more about people than we do—what they need, how they perceive life, what hurts them and causes the violent lashing out against existing conditions.

The testimony of Mr. Wilfred Owen of the Brookings Institution touched on this psychological aspect of the problem, which seems to me a root cause of the whole syndrome. He suggested that we have torn apart great sections of our cities, substituting for human-sized homes a form of "abstract architecture" which is depressing and unfriendly—all right for office buildings, perhaps, but unlivable.

That's where the trouble starts. And then earlier planners made further mistakes—zoning one area for industry, another for commerce, and another for homes. The self-contained neighborhood, which was the mark of the old, livable city, was destroyed. Jane Jacobs, like a prophet, saw it first and described it in 1961. In 1976, Barbara Ward's organization (the International Institute for Environment and Development), published a report based on cities from Hong Kong and Lagos to Boston, tracing the ills of cities to the human distress caused by being uprooted and crowded. The report said—and this is crucial—that crowding is not distressing unless one is among strangers. Crowding in a familiar neighborhood is not objectionable.

A reporter who had come to most of the hearings asked me to sum up my conclusions. They are two: First, we must find out more about human beings, realizing that how things are perceived is as important as how they are: Second, we must study what works and—quite humbly—be willing to correct theory by evidence and try slowly and carefully to create or recreate conditions which make a decent life possible.

Newsletter, *April 21, 1977*

Low-Income Housing Projects

Le Corbusier's idea of urban housing surrounded by open space simply does not work for low-income families. Open space means areas filled with the back seats of cars half burned or ripped out with broken radios and other trash. That's what it means. Dangerous spaces between the buildings, where nobody dares go at night—that's what it means. Fourteen stories depending therefore on elevators, where children stick their bobby pins into the controls so they often don't operate.

The stairs in the high rises can be horrible places. They often have casement windows, which are inappropriate. One day I remember seeing this: Rain had come in and frozen on the stairs, and a thin, exhausted woman was carrying her baby and the groceries up 14 flights of stairs. Residents are lucky if they don't get mugged, on the way up or down. I can't tell you what we've done to people. Four-bedroom apartments with the kitchen 7 by 11 feet.

They were planning another building of this kind in Newark, and I went to Governor Cahill in despair and said, "Governor, you've got to stop it."

He said, "For heaven's sake, Millicent, why are you so excited about this?"

I said, "Governor, have you ever been in one of those places? Have you ever sat down and had a cup of coffee with a woman trying to live in that kind of a place?

"Do you realize that Mrs. Brown has four bedrooms, a big family, and her kitchen is 7 by 11 feet?"

I'll never forget Governor Cahill's reaction. He slapped his hand down hard on the desk, and said, "My God, don't they know anything about living?"

You see, he was a miner's son. And that's what I like about him and other such people. Life at least shouldn't let you forget. What you have been through ought to be of some use to others and yourself. That's the wonderful quality Cahill had. He understood people. He didn't pretend or forget.

I could tell you many stories. I testified in three rent strikes on behalf of the tenants. For instance, they often had no hot water. It would take not just the weekend for repairs, but days and days and days would go by. Nobody would pay any attention to their complaints. Elevators were not repaired. The heating was not working. The incinerators not working. I can't tell you what those people went through. They never should have been put in there in the first place.

Kretschmer Elderly is a senior-citizen project in Newark. It's a splendid high rise, and looks like Park Avenue. But it's for elderly only. It had a man at the front door and you didn't get in unless you were known.

In these other projects life was pitiful. People would only have a small amount of money. They would be mugged going down the stairs to the market. You couldn't get a taxi. One woman said to me, "I tried, you couldn't get a taxi to go into the district, into the area. They said it was too dangerous."

When I first went to my meetings there, I didn't know the way, so I asked a policeman. He said, "You can't go in there at night."

That's how those poor people lived. Under siege. Siege. You can't imagine what it was like.

One day we stopped to visit a project. One of the occupants was a white man who had a small apartment. His door had been broken open by burglars. He had a scar that ran from his ear right down to his shoulder. His wife was in the hospital and he was in despair.

The high-rise, low-income project in one city was finally dynamited—condemned as unfit for human beings. That seems to be the only answer.

Taped interview, September 19, 1980

Health at Home

Mr. Speaker, over one million elderly Americans—5 percent of those who are over 65—live in nursing homes, and many of them will spend the rest of their lives there, isolated from friends and from family members. Although many of these people need the nursing care which can be provided only by an institution, a 1977 Congressional Budget Office study has estimated that 20 to 40 percent of them could be cared for at less intensive levels if funds and adequate community-based facilities were available to them. On January 18, 1979, I introduced a bill, H.R. 1013, which would provide alternatives to institutionalization for these people.

Existing health insurance programs for the aged have a strong institutional bias. Under present medicare law, payments are not permitted for home health care unless the individual has been hospitalized for three days, is deemed eligible for skilled nursing care, or for physical or speech therapy, and is considered "homebound." Medicaid supports the vast bulk of federally subsidized long-term care, yet only a tiny percentage of these funds is used to pay for home health care. With funds available to those who are in institutions, but not to those who might be able to stay home, the incentives all point toward institutionalization, even when this is neither the desired nor the appropriate level of care for the senior citizens.

If some of the money currently used for institutional care could be made available to those individuals or to their families, many could avoid institutionalization altogether. The government would be encouraging family unity, rather than discouraging it. Also, several studies have demonstrated that home health care is considerably less expensive than care in a hospital or skilled nursing facility. In other words, maintaining many elderly people at home instead of sending them to institutions could be accomplished at considerable savings to the taxpayer.

Secretary of Health, Education and Welfare Joseph A. Califano, Jr., has stated that he is "committed to finding workable alternatives to institutionalization." My bill would provide the groundwork for many such alternatives, by authorizing demonstration projects wherein those people eligible for medicare or medicaid nursing home care would be paid a tax-free stipend which they could use to finance alternative forms of care. The stipend, which would be equal to 50 percent of the average nursing home benefits to which they were entitled, would enable these senior citizens to arrange for a home care situation, either with their own or with foster families, with friends or in cooperative arrangements with others, pooling resources. Since eligibility would be based on already established medicaid and medicare guidelines, there would be no danger of abuse or overuse.

For example, an elderly grandmother in my home state of New Jersey, where more than half of the nursing home population is dependent on federal assistance, might be maintained in a nursing home with public funds at a cost of $1,000 per month. With a tax-free stipend of $500—half the cost— she might well be able to stay at home with her family and contribute to the household income. Then her daughter, who perhaps was planning to go to work to help with the grandson's college expenses, would be able to stay at home. Or she might use the stipend to pay for part-time health or nursing care. Any such living arrangement would be reviewed periodically by a registered nurse or other competent official who could determine whether the money was being used to the individual's satisfaction—whether the elderly individual was happy with the situation. A 1977 study by the Urban Health Institute of East Orange has estimated that as many as 35 percent of those senior citizens currently institutionalized in the state of New Jersey might be able to benefit from such an arrangement.

I have introduced the bill with the expectation that while saving a considerable amount of money, it can provide independence and dignity for a great many elderly persons in this country. Separation from one's family or from one's community ought not to be required or encouraged by government regulations and incentives. Institutionalization ought, rather, to be the option of last resort.

Announcing introduction of bill to encourage home
  health care for the elderly
Congressional Record, *April 23, 1979*

Employment

Of all the problems we have had in the last years the most tragic has been unemployment. Congress has tried to address itself to unemployment through a variety of programs, some relying basically on the extension of unemployment benefits, or the establishment of public service jobs; others relying on the concept of public works. Of the two, I think the latter is much to be preferred. The first two are essential as a form of safety net—a system that is used when better methods fail—and I have voted for them for that reason. But what do they really mean? Public service jobs, paying very small wages, mean that people are often working at jobs they have never done before and will never do again when times improve. They are better than extended unemployment compensation, but they are not a satisfactory way of life. And neither, of course, is unemployment compensation.

On the other hand, there is the concept of public works as a way of providing employment when the usual employment in the private sector fails to meet the demand. The great advantages of public works are these: The public—the ordinary citizen who is paying for all the programs anyway—does at least receive a benefit, and often a lasting benefit, from a good public works program. Public buildings in towns where the bonding limit has been reached can be built in this way. Housing, municipal building, sewage treatment plants, and schools would all be eligible. Some might object that the time lag would make many of these jobs come too late to be useful, but the truth is that when unemployment is high and a recession is the cause, many municipalities have had to put off desirable projects only because money was short, because tax receipts were down, and welfare costs up. In the

Fifth District, for example, there were at least five projects, all cleared for environmental zoning and all other regulatory factors, which needed only assurance that the money was available. Among them was a sewage-treatment plant, a senior citizens' housing project, and a multi-family apartment building. The bids could have been advertised the next day, and the whole process started, without adding a single bureaucrat to the rolls. With that, the contractors make profits, pay their taxes, their mortgage payments, and all their usual expenses, and so do the technicians, typists, bookkeepers, professionals, and all the others who are normally employed in projects of this kind.

Money spent in this way generates a great number of subsidiary jobs, in the shops and industries providing services and goods for people who at last have money to spend. I advocated this in the campaign last fall and every day I like it better and better. According to the latest figures, another 1 out of 5.1 of the people employed in the county is paid by tax money. This fact and the growing public assistance rolls, mean an always increasing burden for the workers in the private sector, and one which is not easily cut when times are hard. And there is another point I have always wondered about: Is it wise to wait, as we do, for unemployment to rise to a high, nationwide average level before any move is made to combat it? Would it not be wiser to authorize such public works as this in specific areas which are hard hit? As things are now, a nationwide average means relatively normal employment in some places and tragically high unemployment in others. The "specific area" method would not only bring quicker relief but it might also be more economical, because the wide-spread nature of the "national average" standard demands enormous sums of money. There is some feeling among students of the problems of recessions and unemployment that the effects of unemployment in one place or industry can spread and feed on itself, like a forest fire. It seems sensible to blot it out before it starts.

Newsletter, *July 3, 1975*

Need for a New Approach

Mr. Chairman, if all of us in this House believed that just spending money as we have done in the past would do what we know must be done we would not hesitate. We must give many of our young people, who are coming up to a 40-percent unemployment rate, some hope that there is a place for them in this country. We must be prepared to do so.

Mr. Chairman, I think we must admit that we have learned that we have not yet found a system, and that even enormous sums of money are not going to do it.

We have got to change the ways in which we spend this money and how we administer it.

I can point to two fine CETA programs in my own county of Somerset, New Jersey. I have written to our colleague, the congressman from California, about these two. One was worked out with the labor unions and with cooperating companies, whereby the graduates will receive, if they satisfactorily complete the training program. Department of Labor apprenticeship cards. They are in the mainstream. They will be.

The second is worked out with companies in the district who have devised a special curriculum with our county college. When they graduate and pass those examinations satisfactorily they will receive jobs starting at $10,000 a year.

This is good and this should be emphasized; but on every side we hear the abuses of these programs. What seems to work does not seem to get copied, and too much of it goes into hiring people who are already trained, whom the cities have laid off because they have not enough money to keep them on.

We have seen abuses and we have not yet been able in this House to correct them. We could devise programs for these young people and we should. We are beginning to know now how to do it; but the way we have done it in the past does not work. Millions of them are not employed. Are we going to continue just to pour money down the drain?

I would not mind that as much if we had the money, but first, we don't have the money and second, the young people are not benefiting. That is what's wrong.

We are neither being prudent with other people's money, nor are we giving these young people hope. Now, for so many, there is no hope. That is what I think we have to begin in this House to be concerned about.

Debate on employment programs
Congressional Record, *April 30, 1979*

Contrary to Common Sense

Mr. Chairman, I would like to say what may be surprising to both sides of the aisle:

I approve of extended benefits for those who are truly unemployed. There is no everyday tragedy comparable to losing a job—workers being laid off when they have honestly worked and given their time and the company fails or lays them off, I lost 150 jobs in my district when one plant closed down; 1,500 were laid off in one company and 1,200 in another. We have too many of these. And I am in favor of extended benefits for those honorable workmen. But I do warn this House and the committee, to which I have appealed in vain, that we must have some rational examination of the system. We cannot allow states to have laws which are contrary to common sense in the administration of unemployment compensation.

Now, we have had some changes in my particular state, I will say. Regulations were so obviously unreasonable that we made some changes. But how long are the federal government and the taxpayers of this country going to put up with unreasonable provisions? Furnishing money to help those who are indeed in need and deserve it—I think all would support that. But can we continue without change when we know there are perfectly ridiculous situations beyond any common sense or reason, provisions which, even in one state, provide that a felon who has stolen from the company and for that reason has been dismissed and convicted of that felony, receives unemployment compensation, while on probation or appeal?

Now, how long is this going to go on, before we get the committee, which is charged in this Congress with watching over the interests of this nation and our terrible deficit to do something about it? How long?

I would like to ask the chairman of the subcommittee, if I may: When are we going to consider these things, Mr. Chairman? You know, you and I have discussed them so often.

Debate on extending the duration of unemployment benefits
Congressional Record, *September 20, 1980*

Budget Battle

Mr. Chairman, I am afraid I will have to support the gentleman because I think that is the sensible thing to do. However, I would like to see as much intelligence, urgency, and eloquence raised on behalf of an entirely different procedure which is that we vote on the budget and decide how much we are going to spend, first, the way any family does, and then fit our priorities into what we think we have to spend.

Instead, what we do, is to do it incrementally, starting at the bottom, adding and adding and adding. Then we hit the poor chairman of the Committee on the Budget with the added total which he and our ranking member fight to hold down. But it is the wrong system. Until we get the support of all the authorities in this House to decide, first, what we think this country can afford and then decide where that amount is going to be allocated, we will never have common sense in this House.

Debate on increasing the public debt limit
Congressional Record, *September 26, 1979*

Tax Loopholes

As for the President's tax refund and cut proposals, I question the need for a $1,000 refund for an income of $200,000; the tax cuts for 1975 seem more reasonably allocated. In this connection, I think one of the best parts of the President's address was his reminder that we need fundamental tax reform. We simply cannot continue to live with a system which has so many inequities. It must be changed in such a way that each of us pays a fair share of the burden. It has been said that one man's loophole is another man's livelihood. Even if this is true, it certainly is not fair, because the loophole-livelihood of those who are reaping undeserved benefits can be the economic noose of those who are paying more than they should.

In this regard, I would also like to see the 94th Congress address itself to what has become the most regressive tax of all: the deductions for social security. No one can defend a system in which a married couple with two children, earning $7,000 a year, pays $406 in federal income taxes—and a social security tax of $409.50. I think this is outrageous. If the Congress is truly intent on giving more than lip service to tax reform, we must do something about this at once.

Newsletter, *January 23, 1975*

The Marriage Tax

Mr. Speaker, this week, millions of Americans are filing federal income tax returns, and millions are paying a tax penalty simply because they are married. Today I am introducing a bill to eliminate this discriminatory tax.

Under present law, a husband and wife who both work generally pay more tax than they would if they were single. The Internal Revenue Service has estimated that more than one-half of all taxpayers are married, and at least one-half of all married couples are two-earner couples. This means that one-quarter of all taxpayers—38 million Americans—may be affected by the "tax on marriage."

This bill provides a simple solution by allowing married two-earner couples the option of filing as if they were single. Either spouse may claim deductions for dependents and the child-care tax credit, but they may not be claimed more than once. This remedy will not create a hardship for any other group of taxpayers, as it will only affect those who are subject to the marriage tax.

The tax is now imposed on a married couple if the income of one spouse exceeds 20 percent of the income of the other. The more equal the two incomes, the larger the tax. For example, if each spouse earns $25,000 a year, they pay $2,674 more in taxes than they would if they were single. The tax is especially difficult for low-income families. If each spouse earns $3,750, they pay a "marriage tax" of $168—130 percent more than they would pay if they were living together without being married.

The law should be changed to reflect changing social conditions. In 1950, only 18 percent of married women living with their husbands worked. That figure had increased to 48 percent by 1977. With inflation, more and more couples are finding that two incomes are necessary in order to make ends meet.

Under the present law, if the wife decides to work to help support the family, her first dollar of income will be taxed at the same rate as the last dollar earned by her husband. In effect, her income will be taxed at a much higher rate. This, combined with new expenses for child care, housekeeping services, commuting, and other work-related expenses, creates a real work disincentive.

The present system is designed so that all married couples with the same total income pay the same tax. But the expenses of one and two-earner couples may be quite different, for example, the dollar income of the one-earner couple does not include the value of the homemaker's services.

Other social changes reinforce the need for the bill. The divorce rate doubled in the last decade. The number of households which were shared by unrelated individuals of the opposite sex also doubled—between 1970 and 1977—increasing by a factor of five for those under age 45. The marriage tax penalty encourages this trend.

This simple change in the law would support the family, and it would end one of the most glaring inequities in our present tax system. I first introduced this legislation in 1975; 73 members of the House cosponsored the bill in the last Congress, and a similar bill has been introduced by Senator Mathias and six cosponsors in the Senate. The Joint Committee on Taxation plans to release a report on the "Tax Treatment of Single and Married Taxpayers" in the near future, and Senator Byrd, the chairman of the Senate Finance Subcommittee on Taxation, has promised to hold hearings on the marriage tax this year.

Eleven States, the District of Columbia, and 14 member nations of the Organization of Economic Cooperation and Development now permit or require married taxpayers to file individually. By providing this option to two-earner couples, the bill provides a simple, straightforward solution to a very serious inequity.

***

Extension of remarks after introduction of bill H.R. 3609
Congressional Record, *April 10, 1979*

Taxes Are Punishing the Working Couple

When two working people decide to marry, their federal income tax is usually increased. As soon as one spouse earns at least 20 percent of a married couple's total income, the couple pays a "marriage tax."

For the first time in history, the Bureau of the Census tells us, more than half of all the married women in the country are working. This means that more than half of the nation's married taxpayers—38 million Americans—may be paying the "marriage tax." And experts estimate that, with women entering the work force at a rate of about a million a year from now until 1990, anywhere from two thirds to three quarters of all married women under age 55 will be working by the end of the decade.

The solution to the "marriage tax" exists—we should allow married couples the option of filing separately. We need only to follow the lead of the many states in our union that have two columns on their income tax forms, thereby allowing couples to be taxed individually on their own incomes but avoiding any added auditing or administrative costs. Couples who file in this way would be taxed according to the same rate schedule that currently applies to singles.

In addition, it would eliminate the current disincentive that the "marriage tax" provides to married women who want to work. Under current law, a husband earning $10,000 whose wife does not work pays $707 in federal income tax (assuming he does not itemize deductions). If his wife goes to work for the same salary of $10,000, the effective tax on her income is $2,044 because the couple's tax liability jumps to $2,751. The couple quadruples its tax bill by doubling its income. The United States is the only major industrialized nation in the free world in which the tax cost of the second earner's entry into the work force is higher than that of the first.

On one hand, our government's social policy is to help working women earn equal salaries to those of men, but on the other we have a tax structure that penalizes them when they do so.

The "marriage tax" has other unintended and undesirable side effects. One couple from Maryland flew to the Caribbean three years in a row at year's end, got a divorce, remarried early the next year, and paid for the whole vacation (with money to spare) with the dollars they had saved on their federal income tax.

The Internal Revenue Service caught up with that couple, and their case is currently pending before the U.S. Tax Court, but there are thousands of others who are doing the same thing a little more quietly.

The divorce rate in this country has doubled in the past decade, and the number of unmarried couples living together has risen to 1.3 million, an increase of more than 140 percent since 1970. Each day, I receive letters from young people all over the country who say that they'd like to get married, but they simply can't afford the extra tax.

Our tax system shouldn't be forcing people into cohabitation or divorce. It shouldn't penalize people who get married. When the President took office in 1977, he urged those members of his administration who were living together out of wedlock to get married, extolling the virtues of the family.

In 1980, the same President thinks it will cost too much to eliminate this enormously unpopular and unfair penalty. No responsible member of Congress can advocate a major tax cut that would increase the deficit, but the Congress has just passed a "windfall profits" tax that is expected to raise more than $230 billion, 60 percent of which is to be used to cut income taxes. If a tax cut is to be enacted, justice should be served. The cost of eliminating the "marriage tax" would be only about $5 billion a year.

The time has come to restore fairness to our tax system, and to give the beleaguered family a boost at the same time. We should end the tax on marriage.

The Philadelphia Bulletin, *April 14, 1980*

Energy

In any conservation program, which will inevitably mean sacrifices for all of us, public confidence is the heart of the matter. If conservation is so important, and I believe it is, the public is going to have to be convinced that it is all on the level, that no group is being favored by little clauses in the program that escape the attention of the usual reader, that there is nothing deceptive or false or contrived. We must know that any sacrifices we are asked to make are necessary to a sensible and well-thought-out plan.

For this reason, I am prepared to vote for the objective and impartial investigation of any allegations that are lodged against one section of the economy or another. Are any powerful companies "ripping us off"? Are environmentalists visionary and impractical? Are the government officials inept or corrupt? We must get to the bottom of the rumors, and base our conclusions on facts.

Congress has already voted large sums for research and development in the field of renewable energy sources—solar, wind, water, geothermal, and cogeneration—the total was $1,244,000,000 for the year ending September 30, 1977. I support appropriations for research and development in any field that offers serious hope of practical results, because we cannot continue as we are. We are importing oil at a rate which may well amount to 50 percent of our use very soon, if the present rate continues. This puts our economy at the mercy of foreign countries, which may be raising prices for any political reason. It affects our balance of payments, our cost of living, and the rate of inflation. I am convinced that all of us will support a comprehensive program, even if it does involve sacrifice, if we are convinced that the program is just and sound.

The public is fully aware that everyone in government is not a genius. No one knows the whole truth and even experts make mistakes. But the voters should be able to count on us to tell the truth as far as we can ascertain it. They should be sure that whatever mistakes are made are the result of inevitable human error, not the contrived deceptions of those who want to pamper their own egos or to advance their own interests, rather than the public good. I believe we can have a sensible energy program, supported by public opinion, if it is not only developed in that way, but seen by everyone to have been so devised.

Newsletter, *March 10, 1977*

Common Sense

Mr. Chairman, we have been held up before in this House. We were faced not long ago with an ultimatum—vote $662 million or else—and the "or else" was so terrible. It meant people left helpless without food stamps.

Under that kind of a gun, you have no choice. That is precisely what I think we have to avoid here.

When we think of the suffering of an oil shortage we know what we are talking about. This is not like a war, with an enemy that may attack on any front. It is a gas shortage. Our people know perfectly well what it is. Common sense tells you what is going to happen with a gas shortage or heating-oil shortage or any of these shortages. We know perfectly well what we are dealing with.

As far as a glut is concerned, we can have two million more barrels a day and have a glut. On the other hand, we know what happened when we lost three million barrels a day from Iran.

We cannot be without some kind of a standby plan, and we should be able to handle it here in the House.

We have all heard aspersions cast on the ability of the House to resist the political pressures that one group or another group may subject the members to. But can we say, in all honesty, that we are weaker in resisting pressure than would be one man, a candidate, under pressure to promise one thing to one group or do one thing for one group and not another?

I think the House with its variety of people and variety of

pressures is perhaps a safer place for such a program to be hammered out.

I hope very seriously that we will consider what we do. We must have some common sense in our approach to the problems of the people of this country. The place we can exhibit it is in hammering out the kind of rationing plan we ought to have in the public interest.

I voted for the last standby rationing plan—many in this House did not—in May. I believe we must have one. Surely we ought to stand up and do what we know ought to be done.

Debate on amendment establishing a standby gasoline rationing plan, to be approved by Congress
Congressional Record, _July 31, 1979_

A Formula

Mr. Speaker, we all know it is going to be a terrible hardship with fuel bills this winter, but I would like to remind the House what happened two or three years ago. We had a very hard winter, and we voted funds. Then we found that, as I remember it, the Virgin Islands and Hawaii had gotten more heating money than New Jersey.

What kind of administration is this? What kind of formula is it? We had $100 million left over at the end of the year.

I do not know how we are going to handle the people's money if we have no criteria, no way of handling it, and no way of deciding where the money is going to go before we start handing it out.

Mr. Speaker, I do not wonder that sometimes the public despairs. It is an awful lot of money.

Debate on appropriation to help pay fuel bills for the poor
Congressional Record, *August 2, 1979*

Wilderness Areas

Mr. Chairman, I would like to speak very much in the vein of our colleague, the gentleman from Vermont (Mr. Jeffords). I speak for those of us in the East who have seen the ultimate destruction of almost every single one of our great natural resources through ignorance and through the pressure of population.

Many people in my district are concerned about our wilderness areas in the West. They go there to recapture a great refreshment of the spirit.

I know it is not easy for those of us from the East to speak like this. It is not our land that we are hoping to see designated as wilderness; it is yours. It is yours, those of you who are from the West, and perhaps it is unbecoming for me to speak in this way.

But we are all citizens of this nation, and we are not saying this land will be set aside forever. Sometimes I feel that those who seek to stop wilderness areas feel that we are taking that land away and putting it on another planet.

This does not mean that it will not eventually perhaps have to be used. It just means not now, not yet, and not until it has to be used.

There is a prudence here. There is caution and a conservative approach to the use of the resources of our nation. We cannot live forever in boxes one on top of the other. There has to be some place where we can go and see what God really intended for this world.

Debate on establishment of Central Idaho National Wilderness
Congressional Record, *April 16, 1980*

Realm of the Possible

Mr. Speaker, I rise in support of this compromise. It is states-manlike, I imagine. It is disappointing. It is prudent. It has many virtues. And it lacks many others. But I think it is wise at this moment to support it, and we have to accept that which is possible even if it is not perfect. I congratulate the chairman. I was a cosponsor of the Udall–Evans bill. I regret that this is now before us, but we must accept what we have.

Thank you.

Debate on House–Senate compromise establishing Alaskan wilderness area
Congressional Record, *November 12, 1980*

Environmental Protection

Back in the Fifth District, as your representative I have become involved in new issues and questions, to add to the transportation, employment, and conservation issues which have been in the forefront of concern for all of us. The Dinky and the Central Railroad and the Erie Lackawanna; Picatinny and its 5,700 jobs; the Passaic River and its floods—all these are continuing and vital issues. But a new one was suggested by the mayor of one of our towns: "How does one draw the line between environmental standards and the cost they entail?" At what point does one say, "That is too great a cost for too small a benefit?"

To take a concrete example: Blankville has a sewer system with secondary treatment. To raise that system to tertiary treatment will triple the sewer costs of each homeowner, but the net effect on the stream will be minimal, owing to the pollution of farm and town–street runoff. Many of us would question such a one-sided cost–benefit ratio.

On the other hand, to those of us who have worked for environmental protections for many years and feel strongly about the absolute necessity for high standards, any suggestion that standards need to be relaxed causes a red warning flag to go up. Opponents say we are knee-jerk conservers, and perhaps we are. We worry about special interests and their reasons for advocating changes that weaken the hard-won protections. We cannot have a system so permissive that standards can be relaxed whenever sufficient pressure is built up, nor can we have a system that is unable to accommodate sound considerations of the cost, as compared to the benefits, involved in any special situation.

It was good to find an understanding of this problem in the Department of Environmental Protection. We must develop the ability to exercise hard common sense without surrendering principle. There are going to be cases when the homeowners' sewer costs will have to triple, and no one applauds that; but when the environment is to be protected from a heavily polluting source, there will be times when it will be necessary. On the other hand, no conservationist would insist on such a heavy cost in return for a truly minimum improvement.

It is not easy to make these decisions wisely nor to draw up legislation that will protect us against too much permissiveness and at the same time allow for common sense considerations.

We come, as always, to the dangers which are inherent in any law which allows for judgments on individual cases. The abuses have been legion. Without this flexibility, law is often seen to run quite contrary to common sense, but there is no way to exercise common sense without judgment—that is the problem. It is the art of government, and no one has mastered it perfectly.

This is a controversial matter, of concern to all of us— conservationists, homeowners, and businessmen, as well as legislators. We are all going to have to think about it and make up our minds where the line should be drawn.

Newsletter, *September 18, 1975*

As Advertised?

I would like to comment and to oppose the amendment. Two very interesting things came to light in the debate on the floor of the House. Objection was made to a program entitled "Study of the Sweat Glands of Australian Aborigines." It was considered to be totally irrelevant, but it turned out to be a most important study that the Army wanted because of survival in very hot desert conditions.

Another was a study entitled "Study of the Sex Life of the Fruitfly."

I remember one of our colleagues from Texas rose and said that this study saved millions of dollars for the growers of Texas; that they did not have to spray from airplanes any more. They merely put out attractive little lures with exactly the right kind of perfume, sex-attractive perfume, and solved a great problem for that whole area of Texas.

I think the titling has a lot to do with the discouragement of the public. We must be more accurate.

Thank you.

Debate on amendment to cut funding for the National Science Foundation Congressional Record, *September 5, 1980*

Part 3

CONGRESSIONAL REFORM— A VIEW FROM INSIDE

Power tends to corrupt; absolute power corrupts absolutely.

—Lord Acton

Reform Defeated

Once again, in the House of Representatives, the old ways have prevailed over the forces of reform. As one of our leading newspapers put it, "The political spoilsmen" have had their way. The issue was a regulation of the newly-established Federal Election Commission, which required that the financial campaign reports of candidates for the House be filed with the commission. Reform elements supported the commission's right to do so. Opponents preferred that the old way, filing with the Clerk of the House, be retained.

The issue was not strikingly important in itself. What was important ("an ominous portent for the commission," one newspaper called it) was that the House proved to be unwilling to accept a legitimate and reasonable rule of the body established to regulate campaigns for federal office.

In this first test, the House voted 257 to 148 to disapprove —and thereby nullify—the rule. It was a bipartisan vote and a bipartisan failure—196 Democrats and 61 Republicans voting to nullify the rule; 73 Democrats and 75 Republicans voting to uphold the commission. Of the New Jersey delegation, on the final vote five of the twelve Democrats joined the three Republicans on the commission's side.

It is sad. The country has paid a heavy price for the way our politics have been conducted. We have been angered and shamed to note the large sums that candidates receive from special-interest groups and to trace those contributions straight into the voting records and actions of many political figures.

In reaction to that anger and shame, the first steps toward

election funding reform were made last year. The public had a right to believe that we had all learned a bitter lesson and that the necessary further steps toward reform would soon follow. What does this action of the House tell them now? Does this mean that every time the Election Commission moves to correct a practice it thinks unwise, the House will nullify the rule it finds inconvenient?

We all know the direction our politics must take if we are to correct a potentially corrupting system, a system which permits large contributions from special interests to a candidate's campaign. It is a "potentially corrupting" system, because it is undoubtedly true that many good members of Congress are not tied to those who contribute. They may often vote contrary to the urging of the lobbyist, and they will tell you so. When they do vote as the lobbyist asks, it may well be—and surely often is—because that is the legislator's conviction. But what can the public think, when time after time the big contribution can be stacked up against the voting record? And what of the times when—as every candid member of Congress will tell you—the vote for that particular measure just "had to be"?

No one who has studied the workings of our political system will deny that here is the single most corrupting practice that is still legal.

Newsletter, *November 6, 1975*

Campaign Contributions

Last week's report dealt with the first defeat of the new Federal Election Commission on the floor of the House of Representatives. It was a sad occasion, because it was concerned with the greatest evil we still allow in our political life —the contributions of special-interest groups to our campaigns for federal office. This is the situation we will be facing in the campaigns next year.

$12.5 million have already been collected—$4.5 by the labor unions, $2.5 each by the health and agricultural interests, the rest by educational and other groups. And we know where it's going—into the campaigns for the presidency, the Senate and the House.

The present campaign reform law is only a minimal first step. It prohibits contributions of more than $5,000 to any presidential candidate from any one organization. But this is misleading. Most special-interest groups are divided into national, state, and even county organizations (some proliferate even further), and each one will be allowed the $5,000 maximum. Under the new law, one special-interest organization, concentrating on a presidential candidate, could conceivably arrange to provide for that candidate $255,000 from national and state groups alone. With counties included, it could be the entire $10 million permitted by law.

For candidates of the House, there is a proposal to limit contributions from groups to $70,000 for each election, primary and general, for a total of $140,000—but this will not necessarily reduce dependence on special interests. For the Senate candidates, the proposed limit is tied to the population and other factors, but organizations have a free hand within that sum.

This system must be changed, but it will not be easy to do. It is the system people are accustomed to: It is the way things have always been. Organizations will fight any change because they feel they gain by the present system. The only hope is that the public will begin to believe that the special-interest groups are right—that they *do* gain by it, at public expense.

I hope every "candidates' night" will find citizens asking, as they have every right to do, "What organizations do you accept contributions from, and how much?" Or letters could be sent asking the same questions. When candidates begin to realize that citizens are interested, we may see the beginning of change. The press can reveal these practices and it often has, but until citizens respond and care, nothing will happen. We will go on and on, passing legislation and allowing federal regulations that benefit special groups at public expense.

As one opponent of the federal commission's ruling said on the floor during the debate the other day, "It is all right the way it is." It isn't all right, and everybody knows it. We should be moving toward real election reforms at once.

Newsletter, *November 13, 1975*

Special Interest
and Special Privilege

"On the one hand," said the economist, "you have a problem in macro-economics, and on the other hand . . ." When the economist had left the room, Harry Truman reportedly said: "What I need around here is a one-armed economist."

What the country needs—and most particularly what Congress needs—is a one-armed reformer. Why do we get these "tax-reform" bills without reform, these "Christmas-tree" public service and public works jobs bills, this legislation that opens the door to special privileges for special-interest groups and builds a high wall of protection for certain occupations, costing the public billions of dollars unnecessarily, every year, year after year? And why is it that the legislation that really does try to reform never sees the light of day?

There are two reasons, I believe. The first is that one party, the Democrats, has been in charge of Congress for too many years, and its majority is too big. Its power is enormous, and the arrogance of power infects it. Good people are voting as they shouldn't—against election reform, to take the most obvious example—because the powers of the hierarchy and the committee and subcommittee chairmanships are so seductive.

The so-called "reform Congress" was installed in 1975, but the first act of the Democratic caucus was to confirm Wayne Hays in his chairmanship. The overwhelming majority of Democrats there voted with him in the House to abandon the vestiges of the October 1974 reform, among them one that opened all hearings and meetings of committees to the press and public. In May, only 11 of the 75 new Democratic reformers stood up against Hays and voted to sustain the Election Commission when it presented its first reform to the House.

"If you want to get along," Sam Rayburn is said to have advised a novice, "you have to go along." The temptations of power—to control which bills will be released from committee, and who will be hired, and office space, and all the rest—are soon evident, even to a newcomer.

The second reason we get so many of the wrong bills and so few of the right ones is the money that organizations contribute to election campaigns. No organization, whether professional, business, or occupational, should be allowed to contribute to a candidate or spend money on his behalf. I know that there are many honorable people in Congress who accept such gifts and say—quite truthfully, I am sure—that they vote as the organization wants them to *only* when they think that it's the right way to vote. But I also know, by direct answers to plain questions—"Why are you voting against this disclosure section?" . . . "What are you doing on the veto override?"—that sometimes the motives are mixed. The plain answer that I once got was that so-and-so "wants it and they gave me money." Another time I was told, baldly: "What do you think I'm going to do—I got fifty-eight thousand dollars from those boys?"

Apart from the motives, what about the public—the poor, patient, and now almost totally disillusioned public—which is paying for the whole thing? What can the people think when, thanks to disclosure, the slimy trail from the contribution to the vote can be so easily traced? Just as Harriman and Hill were said to have bought up the legislatures of the West when the trains were going through, so the new special-interest groups are now seen by the public as controlling factors in the votes of the House.

The tragedy is that though some of the finest people I have ever met are in Congress, they are trapped by a terrible system. It is as though our feet were stuck in concrete; we can't get away from "the way things are." In my opinion, the only thing that will cut us loose is a public that understands the evils of the system and demands change. When every candidate is asked—repeatedly—which organizations he or she had accepted money from, and how much, I think we will begin to see some changes. Candidates will see that the voters care.

And, if the voters care, we can get more than half-hearted reform. We got a commission on administrative review to recommend a better system, but, on the other hand, no report is called for until December 31, 1977, so there will be no changes until 1978 at the earliest. We got a suggestion that the commission "should seek the advice" of the General Accounting Office (GAO), but, on the other hand, there was no provision for a mandated audit of committee accounts.

Surely it is time for us, the members of Congress, to work with single-minded purpose for reform. Both parties have been revealed as less than exemplary in their approach to governmental affairs. If these scandals don't move us, what in Heaven's name will? We have a sturdy governmental system—Thomas Jefferson called it "the strongest government on earth." But no system can withstand this kind of abuse forever. We must not only clean house at this time, but in this Bicentennial year we must summon up some of the passion and belief, some of the capacity for self-discipline and sacrifice which carried forward, like a wave, the vision of a just and free society we once had. Above all, perhaps, what we need is courage.

Washington Post, *August 24, 1976*

The "Royalty Complex"

It is time the public and press demanded that the U.S. Congress give up its "royalty complex." President Carter referred to this when he said, soon after his inauguration, "Government officials can't be sensitive to your problems if we are living like royalty here in Washington."

This complex is shown in big ways—the refusal of the House, for example, to allow the Federal Election Commission the right to make random checks of campaign finance returns. And in small ways—the vote to put 25 hairdressers in the Capitol Beauty Shop on the federal payroll, which has risen by 112,000 since January 1, 1977.

Then there's the grossly abused privilege of franking.

From September 1 through September 18 this year the basement corridors of the House office buildings were clogged with five-foot stacks of "newsletters"—campaign brochures, in effect—going out under the franking privilege of members of the House, at a cost to the taxpayers of about $13,000 for each candidate. Photographs of these incumbent-candidates, all running for reelection, adorned each brochure, with accounts of achievements, positions taken, and votes cast.

Under the regulations of the Federal Election Commission, none of these mailings, which go out to about 120,000 to 150,000 "postal patrons" (no names and addresses required) in each congressional district, should be sent out 60 days before the elections, in order to give a nonincumbent challenger (who has no franking privilege) somewhat of an equal chance. But the interpretation of the regulation has been that these mailings need only be presented to the mailing room two days before the legal date, which this year was September 5.

The figures for these mailings are compiled quarterly and the numbers are revealing. For instance, in the last quarter before the required 60-day cutoff in the 1976 election year (July, August, September) a total of 81 million "newsletters" were sent out. In exactly the same quarter (July, August, September), 1977, a nonelection year, some 54 million were mailed. This year, if the members were as busy as usual, the number was probably about 81 million, costing well over $6 million.

All this is legal, but it certainly does not seem right. During the year, the electorate has been bombarded by these newsletters, printing costs having been paid by the allowance each member receives from the Treasury. In off years, when there is no election, a modest number might well be appropriate. Constituents like to hear from their representatives and questionnaires serve the dual purpose of defining issues to the electorate and informing members about the views of the public. But in election years, surely the franking privilege should be limited, and shared after the primary with a challenger who has received a certain proportion of the vote.

To cite another problem, the House has refused to consider the greatest single evil which is still allowed under the federal election laws—the deadly influence of the campaign contributions of special-interest groups. Look at the totals: $12.5 million for the congressional elections of 1974; $22.6 million for 1976; an estimated $30 million for 1978, according to Common Cause.

To whom are they given? To both parties, but primarily to Democrats because that's where the power of the chairmanships lies. Why are they given? Partly as rewards for past favorable votes and in hopes for more in the future.

Some of the finest people in America are members of the House—conscientious, unselfish, and earnestly trying to serve the public faithfully. Many do not take such special-interest group contributions at all; others limit them to $100. But until special-interest gifts are stopped no member who accepts them will be entirely free. The answer is limited expenditures in elections and modest public financing—the best buy the consumers of America could make.

Beyond these aspects of congressional practice lies a problem which the "Koreagate" hearings revealed. According to testimony at a public hearing, a subcommittee chairman of the House Appropriations Committee, Democrat Otto Passman of Louisiana, was able to "persuade" two foreign governments (South Korea and Bangladesh) to nominate the St. John Shipping Co. as broker for the shipping of Food for Peace —P.L. 480—grain to those countries. Two friends of the chairman invested $900 in St. John and made a net profit of $1.7 million in a very short time. This is just one of a number of similar cases, and it shows how tempting the opportunities are.

We have a system which is an invitation to fraud and conflict of interest. That most people resist the temptation is a credit to them, not to the system. But it is extraordinary to find how much resistance there is to any change. People who are beyond suspicion are nevertheless reluctant to face the problems and to consider sensible ways to bring about basic reform.

I remember what the cameraman said to me, after a television interview in which I had talked somewhat in this vein. He said, "I liked what you said, lady, but you're never going to get anywhere. You're talking about a system, and nobody's interested in a system. You've got to get a guy and tell us his name and what he made off with and what you're going to do to him—that's interesting!" I answered that we had done that —Mr. Nixon and Wayne Hays were gone, packed off like scapegoats, but the system which allows and therefore breeds such scandals stands intact.

We do it all the time. We draw up legislation concerning welfare or the CETA program or Title I of the Education Act —program after program—in such a way that it becomes an easy trap. Scandals erupt and the guilty are named and blamed, but the system goes right on. Those who run the programs and often deplore the fraud are afraid that any criticism will result in curtailment of the funds. The fact is that the public is so enraged—and rightly—by the waste and fraud that the scandals will destroy the programs in the end.

In the same way, the scandals the press reveals about Congress have brought about a dangerous contempt for government on the part of the public. Like the cameraman, and for his reasons, the press concentrates on personalities in the fraud news, not on the system. We need to evolve in this country standards of conduct which the public will demand of every public servant. There must be a consensus. We can no longer afford to reelect—as we have—convicted felons or even men in jail.

The need for such a consensus is becoming more and more widely appreciated. We must have a widely based and strongly held view of just what conduct is unacceptable, and what conduct is to be praised. For example, it would be a fine thing if the press would congratulate every president or governor who conspicuously appoints judges and prosecutors without regard to politics. In this way, the public would become accustomed to looking for such actions, and reward such officials with their trust and their vote.

Only the press and the public, working together, can evolve such a consensus on standards. We cannot afford to go on like this much longer. The world, now nerve-tightened by the speed of communications and transportation, is in too tremulous and fragile a condition to allow for a U.S. government so diminished in the respect and confidence of its citizens.

The Christian Science Monitor, *October 5, 1978*

Rich Man's Club,
Poor Man's Temptation

We really can't go on like this. It's impossible. The money that is spent in elections is absolutely unconscionable—even if it's private money. It's true that one's not corrupted by the expenditure of one's own money, but to some extent the system is. We cannot have a system in which the only people you can count on for a vote that doesn't look as though it might be a vote for a special-interest group are people with enormous fortunes.

This year, one candidate for a governorship spent close to $10 million on the campaign and there were not that many people in all of his state; and when a senator ran in another state against an opponent who, despite handsome Political Action Committee (PAC) contributions, could raise only a few hundred thousand dollars, he spent one or two million of his own. He's a fine senator. I say nothing against him. But that's not good. What is the ordinary human being going to do?

This year, a member of the House spent close to a million dollars in his district. He lost. But the point is, that's outrageous, and where does he get the money? From all kinds of out-of-state groups. It's just not good enough. We must get some legislation to control this.

In some ways, the Supreme Court made it more difficult, because they said, under the First Amendment, you have the perfect right to spend as much of your own money as you want. In the presidential election, if you take federal money (taxpayers' money in other words) to run for the presidency, then you, and the groups that contribute to your campaign, can be limited in the amount that you can spend. Maybe what we ought to do is to make it mandatory that anybody who runs for federal office takes some federal, in other words, taxpayers' money.

You know, I've been so lucky. I've had four Democratic opponents now, and three out of the four have been wonderful. Such nice people and such high-level and sometimes hard-fought campaigns. But nice. This last time, I asked my opponent, a young lawyer, "Don't you think it would be good to limit our campaign expenditures? I've stopped all my newsletters so you're not going to have a barrage coming up against you." (Our congressional franking privileges are paid by the taxpayers; and I have introduced a bill to divide it, so that in an election year the franking privileges are limited and divided between the incumbent and that person who represents a party which received a certain percentage of the vote in the election. The bill will never pass. No one will vote for it, but I'm trying to see if we can't move in that direction.)

In any event, he and I agreed to limit our campaign expenditures to $22,500, and we didn't spend that, either of us. And you know, really, that's what we ought to do. My friends keep saying, "Oh well, there's no use. He didn't win, did he, and you had all the advantages of incumbency."

That's true. I also have the disadvantage of a number of votes which have pleased some and not others. Certain people who don't approve of my voting record put fliers under the windshield wipers outside churches. You run up opposition, too, by your votes, especially if you have to take stands on controversial issues, and of course you do. So there are penalties, and if we could somehow even up the advantages, which the franking privilege certainly is, I think we'd do better.

I went to a dinner when Ford was still President, and had my eyes opened. I was in my first term and I hadn't been down here three months. President Ford was planning to veto a certain bill and I asked a young man, one of the so-called Reform Young Democrats, "What are you going to do on the veto override tomorrow?"

And he said, "Oh, Millicent, are you kidding? I took fifty-eight thousand dollars from labor, and they want it."

Representative Les AuCoin told a most interesting story along this line. I mention his name because it was in the newspapers. He gave an interview to *The New York Times Magazine,* so I'm not telling tales out of school. He was in his office when the telephone rang. "How are you, Congressman?" (This was a representative of a group that had given him money.)

"We have a bill we'd like you to cosponsor."

Les AuCoin said, "Well, tell me about it."

So the voice on the telephone said, "Well, for a brief outline . . ."

Les said, "Well, it sounds good. I'd like to see it."

The tone changed and the voice on the telephone said, "Hey, buddy, wait a minute. We're friends, aren't we? We contributed to your campaign? And friends don't ask to see a bill before they cosponsor it."

Need we say more?

Taped interview, January 15, 1981

"Best Congress . . ."

"This is the best Congress that money could buy," said Senator Edward Kennedy, referring to the elections of November 1978. And there has been no improvement since then. The sums of special interest group contributions to Congressional campaigns tell the story.

In 1974, when I was first elected to Congress, the special-interest groups contributed $12.5 million to the congressional campaigns. In 1976, the figure rose to $22.6 million; in 1978 it was $35.2 million; and in 1980, $55.3 million, as reported by Common Cause.

That this imposes a heavy burden on some members is made plain in a speech delivered on the floor of the House by Lloyd Meeds (Democrat from Washington), and reported in the *Congressional Record* of July 19, 1978. Announcing his retirement he said, "Financing is not the only reason. There are other reasons; but the single greatest reason that I will not seek reelection is because I would have to raise $250,000 or thereabouts to run a winning campaign."

He outlined the need to collect such a sum in "big chunks . . . in several instances I raised $10,000 from one source." His speech ended, "As the cost of campaign financing increases and increases we are increasingly going to be called upon to put our souls on the line unless we do something to lessen the private interest that is connected with the donation of funds." I concurred, saying ". . . my colleague . . . is speaking for many of us when he addresses the single greatest legal evil that still exists in our whole election process."

These contributions come from what are now called

"PACs"—Political Action Committees. And they come from almost every section of our economy: 2,500 of them from business, labor, the professions, the agricultural groups and a new category, the ideological groups. A cynical joke refers to this: "A Congressman is held upright by pressure from all sides."

The fact is, however, despite the jokes and cynicism, that many members of Congress accept the contributions and vote their conscience. It just happens that much of the time, the vote and the contribution are in line with the beliefs and the temperament and judgment of the member. The evil of PACs shows in the open admission, without an instant's hesitation, "I took fifty-eight thousand dollars, and they want it." And it shows in the dismay and disappointment of the people, who see the votes following the reports of campaign contributions. No clear conscience, no independent judgment, can wipe out this unfortunate impression.

The inevitable conclusion is that we must reform our election laws. The Supreme Court has decided that when public funds are used in a campaign, Congress can limit the amount spent. (But there are public funds only in presidential campaigns.) Otherwise, the First Amendment free speech clause allows a candidate with a large fortune to spend any amount on the theory of "the public interest." The Court ruled that individual gifts should be limited to $1,000 and PACs to $5,000 in any campaign—primary and general. But there are many corporations, many labor union locals, many professional, trade, and occupational groups, so the total can be huge.

The question surely must be asked: Is this the way we want our system to work? It is so far from the vision of Thomas Jefferson, who believed that men would leave their farms or factories for a short while and return to them in due time. That this is still possible was proved by Gary Myers, turn-foreman in Armco Steel, a Republican. He defeated a 20-year incumbent in the election of 1974 with a campaign fund of $6,500. He was elected and reelected and then retired, to Beaver County, Pennsylvania, and his job at Armco Steel.

In the last analysis, it all depends on the public. If the

people are disgusted by the spectacle of this extravagant expenditure of money, it will dwindle and, eventually, stop. In the right to spend any amount of one's private fortune lies the problem of unfairness: What does the less handsomely endowed candidate do? In the PACs lies the danger of corruption—actual or perceived. It is time for a change.

Newsletter, *October 7, 1981*

Debate on Abscam

I am not qualified to sit as a moral judge. I would not wish to judge on that ground. The investigations of the Justice Department, at least for the people I see, have been the only reassurance, almost, they have somebody that really cares. It has been an immense consolation that somebody seems to be saying that there is no one above the law. I think if any method is contrary to lawful practice, it should be abolished for everybody. I would not like to see the members of the House or the other body exempt from any system that applies to the people of this country as a whole. I do not like to think that there are two laws or sets of laws in this country. And if any citizen of this country is going to be subjected to a certain system, so should we be.

Excerpt from a colloquy on the House floor concerning the Abscam investigation
Congressional Record, *November 21, 1980*

Slush Funds

A very interesting thing happened the other day, just after I had finished taping a TV program in which we had discussed congressional reform. One of the cameramen came up to me and said he approved of my views, "But there's no use attacking the system. You've got to get someone to hang it on."

I know what he means. Naming an individual, bringing the subject down to a concrete example, makes it more vivid and real. But there is a danger in it, because when the individual has been caught and punished, the tendency is to believe that the job has been done, that the evil has been loaded onto the back of the scapegoat and chased into the desert, The truth is, I think, that even without such a specific case, it is obvious that the *system* is hideously wrong. It goes on creating the same problems. Only a high sense of ethics will keep people from doing what is convenient, what is entirely legal and what others are doing every day.

The worst of the system, I used to think, was that special-interest groups could legally contribute to congressional campaigns, and so often the gift could be traced to the vote in favor of that group. I was wrong. These special-interest contributions are indeed a great evil, but at least they are disclosed and limited; foreign governments and nationals cannot subscribe; and the way the money is spent is limited, also, and on record. I was not fully aware of the nature of "office funds," usually called "slush funds." Slush funds are free of the restrictions that apply to campaign contributions. Anyone can give any amount of money to a member of Congress; it doesn't have to be disclosed and it can be spent for anything, just like other income.

Some members use these funds to pay for extra trips to the home district (beyond the 26 trips the taxpayers are providing). Some use them for printing District-wide mailings (but the franking privilege means that these mailings, which cost the public $25,000 each for postage, are postage-free to the member). Some members use the frank to entertain constituents. These are the justifications given, but the press has revealed that they can, and have, been used to pay for a new car for a member's daughter, and personal expenditures of that kind. In such cases, the funds are additional income, pure and simple.

The system that permits this is so obviously wrong that one wonders how it can possibly be legal. Slush funds should be abolished, but at least they must be disclosed. The public should know where they came from and where they went, and the restrictions that apply to campaign gifts should apply to them.

Lecture fees present another danger. One senator was reported to have been paid $10,000 for every speaking engagement by a certain interest group. That has been cut down now, and the limit is a total of $25,000 a year, but it should be lower and the amount for each speech should be limited.*

In the midst of all this gloom, there are two or three encouraging notes that augur well for the future. The first is that the press is beginning to take notice. A recent article described the deceptive pattern of congressional behavior—"voting down pay raises while quietly increasing other benefits that the public knows little about." I objected, without success, to these deceptive maneuvers during debates in the House in 1975 and 1976, but now that the press is aroused the public will know and we well may get action.

The second hopeful note is the Commission on Administrative Review, which is studying all those matters and seems

---

*This was written four years ago and there is no improvement. On the contrary, the Senate can now receive unlimited speaking fees.

determined to produce a sound report. Not long ago, I testified before them on franking privileges and slush funds. Their questions were good and the quality of the members promises well.

Finally, we come to the Ethics Committee, the Committee on Standards of Official Conduct, of which I am a new member. Our job is to consider conflicts of interest and other such matters on the part of members of the House and committee staff. Several questions are already due for investigation, one of them being allegations of gifts by a South Korean national to House members. The encouragement here comes from the quality of the new members Speaker O'Neill has appointed.

The Democrats have an overwhelming majority in the House—292 to 143—and if their leadership is willing to reform the system, we can hope for a real change. It would be helpful if the Speaker and the congressional delegation received letters from citizens, urging prohibition of office funds and organization contributions to campaigns. If the public doesn't care, we won't get very far. But if Congress knows that the people mean business we can really do something useful in the public interest.

Newsletter, *February 17, 1977*

Junkets

Despite all the talk about reform in Congress, little attention has been given to the question of congressional trips—usually called "junkets." They strike many in the press and public as a burden on the taxpayer and an unnecessary prerogative of the members of Congress. The opposite view is that a better-informed member is able to vote more intelligently, and that travel is one of the best ways to widen understanding of complex issues. Dr. Samuel Johnson believed in it. He has been quoted as saying, "The use of traveling is to regulate imagination by reality, and instead of thinking how things may be to see them as they are."

My own view is that every trip at public expense has to be examined separately. Is it necessary? Is it useful? Is some important question involved? I went to Vietnam last year, for example, at the request of the President and the Speaker, as one of a bipartisan group of eight representatives, accompanied by two staff members. It was a hard trip at a crucial moment and I felt no compunction in traveling at the taxpayers' expense. The same was true of a three-day trip to Rome, to act as official "observer" at an international cultural conference. I went alone.

There are other trips which are undertaken by members of Congress as part of an agreement between our government and another government. Such was the trip the Speaker asked me to join in going to Russia and Romania last August. Had I not been planning to visit Europe for a two-week holiday during the recess, it would not have occurred to me to pay my way.

Nor would it have occurred to me to pay my way, had I been one of the five representatives who were sent to Somalia to see if the Soviet Union did indeed have a missile base there. Trips like these are hard-working trips—uncomfortable and entirely useful. A dialogue between a returning staff member and a journalist as reported in the newspaper, is illuminating: Journalist: "Well, how was your trip?" Staff member: "It was 105 degrees in the shade night and day and if anyone calls it a junket I'll punch him in the nose."

That there are other, less worthy trips cannot be denied and I think it is healthy that the press and public take notice of them. It helps to keep the whole system in proportion. Often a trip is borderline, and it is hard to decide whether or not it deserves support by public funds. An invitation by a foreign government is one of these. Even if the relevant committee of Congress and department of the Executive branch feel a public interest will be served, it might be a matter for each member of Congress to decide as a personal matter of discretion and tact.

The trip I took to China during the New Year recess was an example of this last, borderline type. China certainly plays an increasingly important part in our foreign affairs and we were to be guests of the Chinese government, but it seemed to me that this was a voluntary, rather than a mandated trip, as I am not a member of the Committee on Foreign Affairs. I am a member of the International Subcommittee of the Banking Committee, but no work of that committee was involved, so I felt this should be a personal, rather than a taxpayers', trip.

There are other trips which certainly do not seem to be borderline, or questionable, or anything but an outrageous abuse. The press has reported 21 trips to Europe, undertaken within less than two years' time by one subcommittee chairman and "a friend." The public is rightly outraged. Such actions cast the whole system of congressional travel in doubt.

The answer is a mandated audit of committee accounts, as suggested in my last "Report." The committee chairman would then have to justify each trip and certify the costs involved. When this is a matter of public record we will have more restraint, with reassurance to the public as to how their money is being spent. Dr. Samuel Johnson also remarked that imminent execution "sharpens a man's mind wonderfully." Disclosure has the same sharpening effect on the conscience.

Newsletter, *July 22, 1976*

Pork Barrel

Very little has been written about the way members of Congress emphasize what they have done for their constituency and the tendency of voters to reward this by their votes. And what is meant by "doing something" is quite simple: voting and using one's influence in Congress to bring federal funds into the state or district, without regard to the effect on the budget or the general good. Voting for an airplane made in the district, or a dam to be built in the state, without regard to whether or not the plane is the best buy for the taxpayer, or if the dam is needed, is nothing short of irresponsible. When one representative was questioned as to why he had used his very powerful influence on behalf of a special plane engine, the answer was clear: "I'm representing my district." When the President wisely tried to eliminate some very expensive pork-barrel dam projects, it was noted in the press that Colorado, which had no powerful member on the right committee, was the one state where three dams were successfully done away with. As long as "bringing home the bacon" is admired and rewarded by voters, the budget will continue out of balance and deficits will rise.

Newsletter, *March 23, 1978*

Abscam

The people of the United States have suffered two heavy blows recently, one widely reported, the other scarcely noticed. The first was Abscam—the revelation of an investigation conducted by the FBI which involved seven members of Congress in allegations of gross misconduct. After the first shock, a number of questions were asked: How did it happen that this was "leaked"—that this information was made public before indictments were handed down? Was "entrapment" used—were those who had committed no crime enticed by government agents into wrongdoing? If so, the whole investigation might be endangered.

Attorney General Civiletti has told the press that he carefully supervised the conduct of the investigation, bearing in mind previous court decisions as to which actions constitute the kind of entrapment that invalidates a case, no matter how damaging the evidence. The leak is being specially investigated by the Department of Justice. I understand that grand juries are being impaneled to hear the tapes and the other evidence that is said to have been assembled, but it will probably be many months before all the cases come to trial.

Lawyers and law professors discuss endlessly the various fine points of law and procedure that press reports have suggested. Some have objected that the elaborate methods used were unsuitable for an investigation of Congress. Others have hinted that the investigation was purposely leaked lest it be squashed—or even worse, that other important figures might be involved. But for the layman, the anxious and dismayed private citizen, there is only a heavy sense of loss.

While keeping in mind that there is no proof—no indictment even, much less a conviction—it is a terrible blow that such allegations can be made by a responsible government department against members of Congress. Although judgment as to individual guilt or innocence must be suspended, this much can be said: Leaks are intolerable, because some of those alleged to be guilty may be found innocent by the investigators when the cases are completed and may never be brought to trial; second, if the system of investigation was legal—if no illegal entrapment or other method was used—the members of Congress must be prosecuted just as anyone else would be. If this system is lawfully used in criminal investigations of dope peddlers and counterfeiters, it is perfectly proper to use it against members of Congress. We are all equal under the law.

The second blow to Congress concerned the House of Representatives only. A banner headline across the whole front page of a Washington newspaper brought us the news: HOUSE LOSES SECRET BID FOR IMMUNITY. Apparently unknown to any member of the House, the Department of Justice had asked the Clerk of the House in November for certain papers and records of a member. According to the report, this was the sequence of events: The Clerk refused, and a subpoena was delivered; the Clerk refused again and took the case to court; acting together with the attorney for the member, he carried it to the U.S. Supreme Court, asking for a secret hearing.

It is true that the Constitution gives certain immunity to members of Congress: "... for any Speech or Debate in either House, they shall not be questioned in any other Place."

Private records, however, such as bank accounts and press releases, have been open to investigation and to use as evidence. In any case, it was a severe shock to the House to find that we could be involved, through the Clerk and [his counsel] acting as our representatives, in denying a subpoena of the Department of Justice and in asking for secrecy for the proceedings. And all this without a word to any member.

Representative Richard Bolling (Democrat from Missouri), Chairman of the Rules Committee and a leader in past reform efforts in the House, brought a resolution to the floor, asking for an investigation of this bizarre incident. With meticulous and characteristic courtesy and accuracy, he gave credit to the Minority Leader, John Rhodes (Republican from Arizona), as the principal author of the Resolution which posed the investigation as a matter concerning "the honor and dignity of the House." It passed by a vote of 314 to 0. But, except for the Washington newspapers, the whole incident was scarcely reported in the press.

It's bad enough as it stands, but the real significance of this incident is that it leads to so much more: to the attitude of Congress and its employees that members are somehow special, that they will escape the consequences of wrongdoing and be protected from the procedures which apply to all other citizens of this country. And this attitude is essentially an invitation to corruption among the powerful.

There is only one final comment that sums up these events, made by a Frenchman after the fall of France. Corruption is a problem for every government on earth—endemic in every society—but, he said, "My country was destroyed by corruption *without indignation.*" One can only add, ". . . without indignation and without shame."

Newsletter, *March 19, 1980*

Part 4

FOREIGN AFFAIRS

America can neither dominate the world nor escape from it.

—Henry Kissinger

Initiation in Foreign Affairs

As one member of a Congressional delegation of eight, I went to Vietnam and Cambodia on a fact-finding mission. It was a sobering, highly educational experience.

Cambodia gave the first clear lesson. She is so near the tragic conclusion of her drama that the only remaining question is how to achieve an orderly transfer of power, and the basic reality is China.

China supplies arms to the Khmer Rouge, which now controls 80 percent of the country. The tottering government of Marshal Lon Nol cannot last. There must be a structure that will protect the people in the crowded capital, Phnom Penh, and the voluntary agencies caring for them.

But unless this has the backing of China, the killing will continue. The obvious hope is Prince Norodom Sihanouk. He recently sent a cable to the Senate majority leader, Mike Mansfield, offering friendly relations with the United States and amnesty to all Cambodians except Marshal Lon Nol and his closest advisers. This could be the start of a controlled and stable situation.

Marshal Lon Nol intimated his willingness to resign when we met with him. The United States should certainly not be in a position of deposing or installing chiefs of foreign states, but we should at least propose our good offices on behalf of any plan that gives hope of peace.

Further military aid to the Lon Nol government would be useless and might, in fact, be misunderstood as continuing support for Lon Nol and a rebuff to Prince Sihanouk.

Cambodia provided a second lesson. Americans have always given generously to people in trouble. Long before foreign aid was thought of, ordinary citizens were sending help to the victims of war and disaster from Russia to the Yangtze River. Cambodia now shows us that when we give food and medicine to people in need, we should do as much as possible through the voluntary agencies, of which there are such shining examples in Phnom Penh. World Vision, Catholic Relief Services, CARE, and the Lutheran Services are charged with all the responsibility of feeding and caring for these people. The diseases are terrible. Bubonic plague, cholera, pellagra, kwashiorkor, and all other illnesses of malnutrition are rampant.

The children are so famished that they must be fed intravenously before their bodies can accept food. I have never seen or imagined such human suffering and the first thought that comes to mind is "stop the killing."

Vietnam is a far more complicated case than Cambodia because the crisis is farther away, but there is an ominous feeling that Cambodia's fate may sooner or later be duplicated. The people to whom we listened were all opposed to a Communist government. Even those in opposition to President Nguyen Van Thieu, though they hoped to see him out of office, wanted no Communist government. They wanted free elections and were confident that a "third force" would win.

It seems most unlikely that either of these could come along with the victory of the P.R.G. and North Vietnam, but the lesson here is that it must be their choice—not ours. A few days or weeks or years in a country do not give a foreigner the right to believe that any view can be better than that of the people to whom the country belongs.

In the case of both Cambodia and Vietnam, I think we must face the fact that military aid sent from America will not succeed. It will only delay the development of the kind of stable situation—whatever form that takes—that will at least stop the horrible suffering of war. We have no alternative. Those who sent arms to North Vietnam and the Khmer Rouge may well continue to do so for the next thirty years. The citizens of the United States will not. It is not only that we feel we have many problems at home that need attention. It is also a feeling that we should not be in the business of maintaining endless and futile wars.

There will be some who feel that the prestige and status of the United States will suffer in such a denouement. I do not agree. We must have a solid capacity for defense. We must have a clear foreign policy, soundly based on public debate and consensus, about our responsibilities. With these firmly in hand, we should concentrate on a sincere concern for all people, and sensible actions to express that concern. Prestige and status could have no foundation more secure.

The New York Times, *March 21, 1975*

The Public's Role in
Foreign Policy

My report to you this week is going to be about foreign policy because I think it is becoming more obvious every day that this is one of the most urgent questions before us.

A successful foreign policy in a nation where informed citizens have a free vote must be based on a public consensus. Authoritarian governments don't need to consult any electorate or listen to conflicting views. In a totalitarian state, the press is muzzled, and most of the time, the people have no idea where their money is going or what agreements are being made. When Russian tanks and troops went into Czechoslovakia and Hungary to suppress the uprisings, *Pravda* and *Izvestia* reported only that the U.S.S.R. was supporting friendly Socialist states.

We cannot operate this way nor would we want to. But we pay a price for our freedom. Responsible leaders who spend their lives studying foreign affairs may see the necessity for action long before the general public is aware of any problem at all. Swift, timely moves are hard to make unless they are based on a policy already agreed upon, and are clearly seen to be implementing that policy.

It is this gap between the generalized understanding of the public and the detailed information of the expert that makes foreign policy difficult in a democracy. In the philosophical chapters of *War and Peace,* Tolstoi derides the idea that any "leader" really leads. In his view, one who seems to be leading is in fact only expressing a deep and wide "feeling" in the hearts of the people—riding a wave, like a cork in a storm. A leader in a democracy senses the direction of the people's feelings and by giving it expression, intensifies and clarifies it. It is in this way that leadership in democracies is exercised. If this is true, it is obviously the duty of anyone in a responsible position to open a debate on urgent public issues, to draw the attention of citizens to the problem, so that a public consensus can develop.

Now we have come to the point where our foreign policy clearly needs debate and clarification. What are our national interests? Which are vital and which peripheral? What are we prepared to sacrifice for—and by sacrifice, one means, of course, risking all-out war when every way of invoking international cooperation and mediation has failed. The Monroe Doctrine was for a long time the only stated outline of our national interests, but it was based on the tacit understanding that the British Navy would keep other nations out of the Western Hemisphere. In fact, at the time, Britain wanted to make it a joint declaration; the American president made it a unilateral one.

Is the Monroe Doctrine still valid? Are we prepared to go to war, if necessary, to defend every inch of the Western Hemisphere? As for me, this is my first, tentative outline of vital national interests as I see them: Western Europe; the Mediterranean; Canada; the Caribbean; Japan. Should we go further? The Philippines? Korea? Taiwan, where I hope a plebiscite will decide what 14 million Taiwanese want? Australia? New Zealand? The Persian Gulf?

Experts, and the general public, too, may call this list simplistic, even dangerous, in that any area not included automatically becomes an easy target for aggression. But I am not deciding foreign policy. I'm not even a member of the International Relations Committee of the House of Representatives. I am only trying to encourage debate on the questions raised here. It is simply the duty of *all* of us—certainly all of us in Congress—and more widely, all citizens to begin thinking of these questions.

One final word: I hope the public will not encourage Congress to go much further into the implementation of foreign policy—as distinct from its basic outline. The power of the purse, the power of legislative fiat—these are blunt instruments for the delicate operation of diplomatic interchange. It's like trying to open a china box with a crowbar, or untie a knot with your foot. If we are to have a successful foreign policy, it will have to be soundly based and expertly implemented and this needs mutual trust between Congress and any administration. Congressional leaders must be told the truth and the secretary of state must be able to count on these leaders not to "leak." It is a sad thing when we discover, as we have recently, that it is the press—not the political branch —which seems to be the most responsible element, holding information when it is in the national interest, at that time, to do so. But perhaps this question of "leaks" should be the subject of another report. When is a leak not a leak? For this time, foreign policy is the question and I hope to have your ideas soon.

Newsletter, *April 24, 1975*

Tug of War

The other day, Mr. (Paul) Warnke discussed the SALT talks in which he had participated in Moscow. He spoke so frankly about the numbers and the various types of weapons, both in the Soviet Union's arsenal and in our own, that I was astonished and delighted. Not being a member of the Armed Services Committee, I had never before heard this kind of information presented in such clear and straightforward language, under the close questioning of knowledgeable people.

These were some of my conclusions: If either the Soviet Union or the United States has the ability to retaliate, after a nuclear attack, with a number of warheads sufficient to eliminate all essential targets, an extra number of missiles is valuable mainly as reassurance to allies or as a prestige or status symbol to the rest of the world. Another conclusion was that the President's emphasis on human rights did not adversely affect the course of negotiations. After one angry but rather *pro forma* speech on the subject by one of the Soviet Union's representatives, the talks apparently continued in a relatively agreeable atmosphere. The burden of producing large numbers of weapons is heavy on both sides. The SALT talks lead to what is a recognized mutual benefit —a limit certainly, and a reduction if possible, in the arms of both sides. But the argument one often hears, "Why spend so much on arms—there are enough bombs now to kill each person twice," is revealed as entirely pointless. It is not the production of bombs which is so expensive, it is the increasingly sophisticated delivery systems and the development of protective devices. When one side invents a way of shooting satellites out of the air, the other works on a more sophisticated satellite. The sad thing is to see so much human intelligence and ingenuity—and so much time—devoted to such ends. It makes even arms limitation seem essential, and reduction the beginning of a new day.

It was surprising to learn that the Soviets were so willing to talk about the numbers of each type of weapon that they are currently producing and deploying, but I suppose the accuracy of present inspection methods is not disputed by either side, so the usual secrecy is now somewhat out of fashion.

It was interesting to see how simply the equation can come down to a level that would be familiar to any referee of a high school tug-of-war: The Soviets are reluctant to give up any of their heavyweights, the weapons that can carry such big loads of lethal material; and we will not give up our agile, accurate, and speedy delivery systems. They have to be equated, in order to preserve the deterrence that is the best hope of peace.

Newsletter, *May 5, 1977*

Advice to Secretary of State Muskie

To have accepted appointment as secretary of state, given the condition of world affairs and in the wake of former Secretary of State Cyrus Vance's resignation, is the mark of a courageous man. There are, however, a few thoughts I would like to bring to your attention, as a member of the House Committee on Foreign Affairs.

We very much need to hear our foreign policy explained and proclaimed by only one voice, other than that of the President himself. It is confusing for us here in Congress, for the country, and for foreign governments to have a variety of official foreign policy spokesmen. Compounding the confusion are the vacillations and sudden turns of our foreign policy course. There is no general sense that we have a steady goal in world affairs and a coherent, well-understood policy as to how that goal might be reached. We may well have to be flexible in handling special circumstances or crises as they arise, but underneath that flexibility we must have a steady, known purpose, fully discussed in private with our allies, well expressed publicly, by one clear voice, to the rest of the world.

Concerning relations with our allies, we must be honest with them—explaining our view of world events and issues, being frank about what we intend to do and what we hope they might do. We cannot expect that sovereign nations will agree happily with sudden announcements from this side of the ocean that involve and sometimes oppose their interests when they have not been consulted. It is true that often our allies seem to regard an international event, such as the invasion of Afghanistan, as primarily a U.S. rather than a European problem as well. This is hard for us, but our failure to consult our allies encourages this point of view.

Recently, our consultations with our allies have been clumsy or nonexistent. In this election year, we cannot afford to add to their uneasy suspicion that announcements or actions that may further trouble the fragile structure of world peace are based more on the exigencies of American politics than on a sound analysis of the international situation. In fact, our own country needs reassurance about this too. We have seen too many television interviews timed to primary elections; we have heard too many speeches—whether on foreign policy maneuvers or federal funding—apparently designed as a reaction to the polls or to some local politician's support for the administration. This sort of thing is damaging at home, but it is a disaster in foreign affairs.

It is probably unnecessary to stress to one who knows the Senate so well the importance of candor and straight dealing in relations with Congress. As members, we struggle with an almost endless variety of legislation. We draw it up carefully, but we often discover that the State Department has found a loophole and that our intent has thus been avoided.

This experience may teach us to write tighter laws, but there is no way for us to legislate what we most need—the truth. We must be able to count on representatives of the executive departments to tell us the truth as best they can discern it. Too often we are unhappily aware that executive representatives are telling us only what they have reason to believe we already know.

Selective analysis, however, is not confined to the information that State Department officials are willing to give Congress. Reports that do not accord with the position a particular embassy wishes to take are frequently censored before they are cabled to Washington. The effect of this is to make intelligent decisions both by the executive and Congress almost impossible.

For all these reasons, Mr. Secretary, there is a widespread hope that from that beautiful office of yours, you will speak firmly to the whole department, demanding that anyone who speaks for you speaks truthfully. If these are matters that for good reasons of discretion and diplomacy cannot be discussed in public, far better to ask for a closed-door hearing in Congress than to leave a false impression. Foreigners, too, understand discretion provided it does not turn out to have been deception.

The position of the United States is so central to world peace that there is an almost desperate need—here and abroad, in Congress and among all citizens—for a single consistent vision of what our foreign policy is. We cannot afford vacillation, double talk, and sudden surprises. The powers of our government are wisely divided, but there must be honest dealing between Congress and the executive. And in view of the chaos that has infected so many areas of the world, surely our allies, too, deserve a government that works with others in good faith and speaks with a single voice in defining a steady and consistent purpose. It is indeed a happy portent, Mr. Secretary, that your 22 years in public service have shown that none of this is foreign to you.

Foreign Policy, *Summer 1980*

Political Asylum

Mr. Speaker, I had not intended to speak, but the eloquence of the previous speaker moves me to say that I believe that every member in this House cares about our country, that any threat to our country is a matter of tremendous concern to each one of us, and that there are different ways, maybe equally intelligent, of looking at what our interests are.

It would seem to me it would have been much better, a year and a half ago, if that poor boy, 16 years old, whose father had just been killed, murdered by Somoza's men, had been allowed asylum in our embassy. Maybe then we would not have had so many moderate businessmen killed, so many moderate industrialists and sensible people ousted from the country. That is where our interests may lie—in being honestly concerned when terrible injustices are being done. Not with arms, not with money, but with some indication that we understand that something is wrong.

I think we have to reexamine where our interests are. They are not always in shutting our doors when a child, whose father has been murdered, comes to us for asylum. This is not going to be the way. We are going to have to pay some attention to responsible businessmen who are telling us, "Look out." When editors of great newspapers are killed something is going wrong, and it is not wise to continue to close our doors and shut our ears to what is being done to people in this world. We are going to have to reexamine our ways and not stay on every bandwagon until it brings us to disaster, down with the governments that fall.

Debate on providing economic aid to Nicaragua
Congressional Record, *August 2, 1979*

After Helsinki

This report is about a resolution I introduced in the House some time ago which could benefit from your support now.

Last year, 35 nations, including the United States, signed the Final Act of the European Conference on Security and Cooperation—usually known as the Helsinki Accord. Not long afterwards, I went to Russia with a delegation from the House of Representatives and, for me, a somewhat distant and theoretical exercise in international diplomacy became a dramatically present and personal issue.

The change came from seeing the people in Russia and, later, in Romania—the dissidents, the "refuseniks," the Jews and Baptists and Catholics and Lutherans—the lost, helpless people, anxiously waiting for exit visas, for news of imprisoned husbands, for the next visit of the dreaded secret police. Their faces are unforgettable.

It is as different to see these people in the midst of their isolation and fright as it is to come upon an accident on the highway instead of reading about it in the newspaper. As American visitors, however official, we had nothing to offer them but recognition, and it was touching to me how much this meant to them. They were anxious to give their names and addresses and occupations, as though this in itself constituted a sort of lifeline, a change of status away from that of a numbered victim in a nameless list, to that of an individual, known and recognized.

And so it was that we all—victims and official visitors alike

—turned to the Helsinki accord and its promises for human rights in so-called "Basket 3," the section covering the reunification of families, freedom of movement, freedom of journalists, and such concerns.

When I came home and Congress reconvened in September, I prepared at once a resolution to set up a commission to monitor compliance with the accords. Before Congress takes any action or makes any changes in trade conditions, it seems important that Congress should know—directly, and from a source solely concerned with Basket 3 provisions—exactly what each nation is doing to honor the agreements so solemnly made.

There are now over 70 cosponsors of this resolution in the House of Representatives, and Senator Case of New Jersey has entered a similar bill in the Senate. Action in the House was delayed until the Military Aid bill went safely through the Committees and the vote on the floor, but now that this hurdle has been passed, action should come quickly. It is to be considered by the Subcommittee on International Political and Military Affairs in the House Committee on International Relations. In the Senate it is in the Committee on Foreign Relations, of which Senator Case is a member.

When the commission is working we will have one central place where all the information about these Basket 3 provisions can be gathered together. We will know—even if the nations don't like to admit it—more officially, whether or not a liberalized trend is developing. We will know what is happening to the Ukrainians, the Baltic peoples, the Jews and Anabaptists of Russia; to the Poles, Hungarians, Czechs, and Bulgarians; and in Romania, to the Germans, Hungarians, Baptists, Catholics, and Jews. We should know if there is hope for all the people we met, and the millions we never knew, or if there is nothing for them but the prison that refuses to let them go, that dismisses them from any employment as soon as a visa is requested and then jails them as parasites.

No nation now can say that these considerations are internal affairs, out of bounds for the concern or comment of other nations. For the 35 countries which signed, they are matters of international agreement. The accords were signed and they must be honored. Détente must not be bought at the expense of such suffering and injustice.

Newsletter, *March 25, 1976*

Madrid Conference

The international conference, which is meeting in Madrid to discuss human rights and other matters, is supposed to review and report on compliance with the terms of the pact signed at Helsinki in 1975 by 35 nations. The delegation from the U.S. Congress, members of the congressional "Helsinki Commission," spent the Thanksgiving recess there, but this can only be an interim report since the Conference on Security and Cooperation in Europe will not end until February, if the present plan is followed. The final report, in other words, cannot yet be written, but the "review" can be outlined.

There are three sections to the Helsinki pact: military, economic, and human rights. When we were in Madrid, human rights were on the agenda. It is entirely fair to say that the Soviet Union and its allies did everything parliamentarily possible to delay and frustrate any orderly discussion.

The standard Soviet speech, taking an hour or more, was simply "The Soviet Union has complied with all Basket (section) 3 provisions: Emphasis on these concerns is only an effort against détente." This was particularly outrageous in a city crowded with representatives of deprived and suffering groups: Balts, Ukrainians, Roman Catholics, Lutherans, Pentecostalists, Jews. Denied the right of self-determination promised them, the right of family reunification, of religious freedom, of travel, and information, these people hung like a cloud over all the proceedings of the conference. So did the people of Afghanistan, their country invaded in direct violation of the terms of the pact, and so did the workers in Poland, wondering if Soviet troops and tanks might soon be launched against them.

The reaction of free nations was instant and clear. The Netherlands: "We are blamed for damaging détente when we plead for implementation of Basket Three—but are we to blame? . . . So long as some countries equate standing up for human rights as disloyal to the pact, so long will dissension continue." Portugal: "The whole CSCE (the pact) is endangered by these continued violations." And so said Canada, the United Kingdom, Ireland, Belgium, and many others. In plenary session, U.S. Ambassador Jerome Shestack made a strong speech giving specific examples of Soviet violations, naming individuals whose suffering exemplified the depth and variety of the problems: "Names are symbolic . . . the human face of détente."

The Soviet Union demanded the right of rebuttal to Ambassador Shestack's speech and the assemblage stiffened in expectation of an angry reply. But the rebuttal was considered mild, when the Soviet representative said only that they were "surprised" that the United States could rely on the opinions of dissidents and give a speech "containing the names of criminals convicted under Soviet law." Such direct rebuttals were rare, however. Usually, procedural questions were raised in order to avoid any further substantive matters.

In the end, one can well ask, what will be the result of all this? Are these conferences worthwhile? I think the answer is overwhelmingly that they are, for several reasons:

1. They consolidate and unify the Western European nations, Canada, and the United States by driving them together in defense of common values. The division was clear on one side, those who believe that each individual has rights the state cannot take away, and on the other, those who believe that the state can sacrifice every individual whenever it pleases.

2. They strengthen the NATO ties.

3. They demonstrate the fact that concern for human rights

is not an American issue, and certainly not a partisan issue even in the United States, as the Pact was signed by President Ford and the enabling legislation for the congressional Helsinki Commission was drawn up by members who had never heard of the former governor of Georgia.

4. They hold up before the Soviet Union and its allies a mirror in which they can see themselves in the light of ordinary public opinion. It is obvious that the Soviet Union and its allies want—and perhaps even desperately need—détente as long as it means trade. But slowly, year by year, they are forced to admit the judgment of others as enunciated by Anne Anderson, the admired delegate from Ireland: "Human rights are the base and reason for détente."

Like a tide that seems unchanging when one watches it, there is reason to hope that progress in human rights, as measured in these periodic review conferences, will be seen to be inching forward year by year, filling the hollows and covering the stones of cruelty and repression. Human rights are the standard and banner of the West, the inevitable direction, one must believe, of all human societies.

Newsletter, *December 17, 1980*

Human Rights

I started the Helsinki Commission, to monitor compliance with the Helsinki pact, with particular reference to the Human Rights Section, which of course involves the Soviet Union and the countries of Eastern Europe as well as Western Europe and ourselves and the Vatican and Malta, but some people are surprised because I wrote to the South Korean ambassador and the Taiwanese ambassador and the Argentine ambassador about abuse of human rights in those countries. How can they be surprised? Either you mean it or you don't. This is what bothers me.

(Jacobo) Timerman said something very much to this point. I had been writing the Argentine ambassador on his behalf, and so, when he was able to get out, I saw him here at the Capitol. He wrote this in the *Times* and I copied it down:

> Whether it is a minuscule authoritarian country such as Uruguay, or a colossal authoritarian country such as China, the surest way to arrive at and stay in power is the unlimited destruction of human rights.

Now, that's the truth. That's the lesson of the twentieth century. And it's a horrible lesson. It has been transmitted by our remarkable and beautifully developed technological communication system, so that everybody knows exactly what to do. Terrorism and oppression are an airborne infection, a terrible epidemic. Is there an abuse you want to correct? Here's how to do it: Seize the embassy, kill them, or throw them out of the window.

We're not learning the right lesson. And that's the tragedy

of this century, which was supposed to be one of enlighten-
ment, with everybody learning how to read and write, everybody learning how to have better health. What have we
done? As one of the trustees of the Rockefeller Foundation
said, "Ah, what a mistake we made when we went first after
health instead of agriculture."

A terrible thing to say. But profound, profound. They go
hand in hand. The only people who should be in government
are those who care more about people than they do about
power. This is one of the lessons we ought to be learning. In
the long run, everything depends on exactly what you're
after. If you're after power, that's one thing, and then of
course, you've discovered the easiest way, as Timerman has
said, to arrive at power and stay in it. It's just that simple. You
don't have to find out whether they want guns or butter, a
refrigerator instead of a tank. You simply build a tank. You
make 50 tanks, so that they never get a refrigerator.

We're leaning on that broken and pitiful reed, the United
Nations. We hoped for too much from it, I guess. But what a
disappointment. Justice and truth—they don't, they can't, prevail here. The people there are talking and writing for home
consumption, and, so, it still continues, this endless cloaking
of the real drive, in all kinds of high words.

Consider a person like Prime Minister (Michael M.) Manley. Compare him to (J.M.G. Tom) Adams, Prime Minister of
the Barbados. Mr. Adams came here the other day, a very
impressive man. What's he really concerned about? I do believe, and I may be wrong, that he cares most about the
welfare of his people. Why? Because that's what interests
him, that's what he was talking about—the education and
housing and health and jobs of his people.

On the other hand, Mr. Manley wants socialism. He wants
a new system. A little group of about six of us were meeting
with him and he told us that he wept because he couldn't
send troops to Angola with the Cubans. To even think of such
a thing, when Jamaica is in the condition that it's in, is absolutely beyond belief. He seemed to want to be a world figure.
One way of discovering where an individual really wants to

go is to listen. What does he talk about when he has an opportunity to speak?

I said, "Mr. Prime Minister, why do you hope for socialism, since it's proved to be so unproductive? For instance, in agriculture, there isn't a Communist country that hasn't discovered it cannot get collectivized agriculture to be as productive as was farming before it was collectivized. Whether it's the Soviet Union or Hungary or any place else in the world, even the Communist countries have had to admit it. Socialist industrial production doesn't work, either. Now, even Poland is allowing businessmen to have—as in Romania and East Germany—joint ventures. The sellers can go to the plant and see what machinery fits there. Before that, when they talked to the central ministry they found that the central ministry had never been to the plant either, so they would order a whole lot of machines that couldn't get through the doors without tearing down the walls."

And Michael Manley said, "That's a hard question you ask me," and he was very ruffled. Later he said, "You've been very provocative," or something.

Well, I was sorry, but I was trying to find another ruler who really cared about his own people.

No wonder Mr. Manley is having trouble. I met a Jamaican who happens to live two doors away from me, here in Washington. He has family still in Jamaica and goes back there. He said, "I'm beginning to despair. The people who used to run a very productive and high-paying industry—with good jobs, good profits to the country—the bauxite industry, were all thrown out of their jobs. Now no one knows how to run it. It's a mess. The fruit from the collectivized farms—a small crop, smaller than usual, but they forgot to order the boxes, so they couldn't even export that."

He said, "I don't know what's going to happen to that place. The unrest in Kingston is such that they've had to put up a garrison prison for the dissenters."

Mr. Manley had spoken of 300 years of exploitation by the British. Great wealth had been extracted. "Now," he said, "we have terrible problems; we need help, because ninety-four percent of our energy comes from outside the country in the form of oil, and we simply have to pay these tremendous prices for it."

I said, "Well, at least you can't blame us for that. We're not exporting oil to you."

And then he went on and talked about the Third World and its demands, and he said, "But of course we have the great weapon of OPEC."

I said, "But OPEC is what's causing your terrible problems with energy costs, isn't it, Mr. Prime Minister?"

"Ah," he said, "but it's causing much more harm to the industrialized West."

See? That's why it's his weapon, because it's a weapon against us.

Now what do they really mean? They need aid and we must help them but, let's be honest. They call it "transfer of resources," but that means grants from the industrialized countries. And they get them. And what's the result? They don't profit from the aid or learn any lessons from it as to what system is productive.

They say our system is so exploitative. They can't seem to accept the fact that our system has done better for our people than any other.

I remember when Khrushchev was on the Pulaski Skyway in New Jersey, and drove past the Kearny plant parking lot of Western Electric. He said, "What's that, an automobile factory?"

"No, no, that's Western Electric. They make telephone sets for the telephone companies."

"Oh," he said, "all those automobiles? I don't believe you."

So they got off the Pulaski Skyway, thank God, and went there, and they saw that they were indeed making telephone sets, and that all those automobiles belonged to the workers. Incomprehensible to him. And to my mind a simply glorious incident.

I tell you, it's a funny world. Time after time, the proof is there, and people simply don't want to accept it. I don't know what it is. Is it that human beings, in any society, have this strange vision of something far better? And, therefore, no matter what a society produces, in the way of distribution of goods for its children, it isn't enough?

They keep the dream, and although Communism has been proved to be far worse, more exploitative, more repressive, more destructive of human rights than any other system, it doesn't make any difference. For them, there isn't any other dream.

Taped Interview, February 4, 1980

Terrorists

The year-end recess of the House has provided a rare opportunity: a time to read and think, as well as time to go to local
meetings and discuss district problems. Among the local
problems of priority have been senior-citizen housing in
Bound Brook and the secondary sewer-treatment plants of
ten Morris and Somerset county towns. But there has been
time to read, too.

One of the most interesting books has been Jean-François
Revel's *The Totalitarian Temptation,* and among the most
interesting articles was "The Pressures of Liberalism and
Terrorism in West Germany," by Fritz Stern.

Revel is French, a former University professor—a passionate anti-communist, "anti-Stalinist" by his definition—and
his book is a tirade against extremists of Right or Left, but
also against the Center–Left, which by its refusal to stick to
democratic values and condemn right and left equally, makes
the creeping advance of "Stalinism" more and more possible.
His book has flashes of humor, as when he describes the
fanatics of both sides shouting "Death to the extremists."

Stern has no humor, at least not in this sober article in *The
New York Times.* He is a professor of history at Columbia
University and has published a book on Bismarck and the
building of the German Empire. He writes in the article of the
horrors and dangers of terrorism in the Federal Republic—
horrors because all terrorism is ugly in its violence; and dangers because democratic procedures and guaranties of individual rights are strained by the political pressures of an
increasingly outraged and frightened public.

These dangers are growing daily in Italy, also, where political assassination, kidnapping and bombing have become daily occurrences. One remembers the riots and disturbances in Germany and Italy after the First World War and the dictatorships that followed. People are exhausted by continued violence and disorder, and the resulting uncertainty and dangers of ordinary, daily life. As one taxi driver in Rome said to me recently, "I don't care what party wins—we must have order."

A dictatorship can handle dissent by concentration camps, "thought-reformation" camps, "psychiatric" hospitals, and all the paraphernalia of force, because these are understood as possibilities in any system that puts the security of the "state" (this usually means the "apparatus," the ruling élite) above the rights of the individual. A democratic society must look for its defense to those who are truly devoted to the principle of individual rights, which means fair trials and adequate defense for everyone, including terrorists.

The terrorists rail against "the system," but rush to avail themselves of its protections whenever they are caught. Destruction of the system is their constant theme. No matter how varied the conditions in the free countries where terrorism flourishes, "the system" is what they want to destroy.

In this frantic atmosphere the temper of the general public is sorely tried. And this is where Stern's article and Revel's book come together, I believe. Both are calling out to the Center, Revel insisting on greater intellectual honesty, Stern appealing for a steadfast fidelity to democratic values. One is reminded of Yeats' prophetic poem, "Things fall apart, the center cannot hold. Mere anarchy is loosed upon the world. . . . The best lack all conviction, and the worst are full of passionate intensity."

Revel insists those of good will who profess to believe in constitutional guaranties should judge dictatorships of both right and left by the same standard. Stern writes of John McCloy's great contribution in the early days of the German Republic, which has now succeeded in attracting "men and women of ability, passion and responsibility—with a commitment to democracy and the rule of law."

We who are citizens of the United States have to live in a world where all this is happening, where violence seems every day more prevalent in one country and continent after another. We must strengthen—deliberately—our inner defenses against the fashion of excusing extremists of right or left and, above all, against any departures from our rule of law.

It's not an easy world, now that communications and transportation have made it so small, but our Constitution and our independent judiciary are indispensable protections; the free press can be counted on to alert us when they are threatened. Our job is to respond.

Newsletter, *January 12, 1977*

Victims

Mr. Speaker, I would like to join with those who spoke here earlier this morning concerning the plight of Soviet Jewry. I do not think we really understand how terrible it is until we listen to some of the people who have been caught in the claws of injustice.

It was a president from New Jersey who said the business of government is justice. We see what injustices a government can exert upon its own people who are only exercising what should be their rights because their government has agreed to them: the right to travel freely from one place to another for personal or professional reasons, the right to be united with your family—rights that were guaranteed in the act signed in Helsinki on August 1, 1975. These people are asking nothing more than that, and for that they are thrown out of their jobs; they are declared parasites; they are put into prison under the most horrible conditions.

What do we say? How is it possible for this to continue year after year? You have heard the names of the people. You have heard the names of famous people, and those otherwise unknown. We must speak for them all.

Debate on the plight of Soviet Jewry
Congressional Record, *April 5, 1979*

I would like to add my voice to those we have heard here. Dr. Brailovsky is a distinguished man, but I think we have all learned some lessons in this century, and that is that until we can care with equal passion for those who are not so famous, not so well known, the famous will never be safe. Whether it is a matter of terrorism or assassination, until we stand together as human beings, consoling and helping, and where we can rescuing the helpless, we will never do well by the leaders and the distinguished people of this world.

I think of all the people who have come before our commission, of which my colleague from Florida (Mr. Fascell) is chairman. I remember a young Jewish girl who had been in prison because she had tried to help some Pentecostalists. The parents had been in prison because they tried to teach their children their religion. I remember all the many figures, including Amalrik, who was so tragically killed before the Helsinki Conference in Madrid. These figures pass before us, and now here is another one, ill, and there is nothing we can do except to speak here and to urge every person in this country who belongs to any kind of an organization to get their organization also to write on his behalf. Whether they are groups of engineers, architects, scientists, or computer scientists, any organization, has great influence, I have found, in the Soviet Union. That is what we ought to mobilize here, something that we know is effective.

But we must also do this for the not so famous if we want to see justice in this world. This new empire—the Soviet Union—does not send people to be slaves in the ships as ancient empires did. It sends them to the psychiatric hospital or to prison. And this is what has happened to Dr. Brailovsky.

Debate on the release of Victor Brailovsky, Soviet dissident
Congressional Record, *April 7, 1981*

Yes, Mr. Speaker, we are speaking especially today of Andrei Sakharov who has been rightly described as the conscience of the Soviet Union. However, there are so many others. There is Shcharansky, Orlov, Deke, Rudanko, Petkos.

I could recite them one after the other. They are lost in the prisons of Russia or in their psychiatric hospitals, beaten down. I do not know how many members of this House have ever seen a person come out of a psychiatric hospital. Michael Bianstov, too. For two and a half years he could neither walk nor talk when he came out.

That is what Mr. Sakharov is trying to tell us about. That is why it is such a sorrowful day to lose a powerful voice like that. He speaks to us still through his brave wife but how long is she going to be allowed to come and communicate with the Western journalists in Moscow?

They slipped off the train, she and another woman, the other day. Will they be watched so carefully that they cannot do that again?

I think maybe we ought to remember that tens of thousands are lost and never known. They are unknown and unsung names and they die and suffer.

Perhaps Jacobo Timerman who has just escaped from another kind of dictatorship said something that we all should remember:

> Whether it is in a minuscule, rightist country or an immense leftist country, the simplest formula for arriving at and staying in power is the unlimited destruction of human rights.

That is what we are talking about: the unlimited destruction of human rights. These people who have suffered in one way or another, in one country or another, all over the world, are telling us what this terrible century is like.

Mr. Speaker, certainly we should have learned one thing from the 1930s, that if we do not speak up, those of us who are safe and comfortable here, when people are being brutalized by their own governments, we are losing our souls.

I thank you, Mr. Speaker.

Debate on the release of Andrei Sakharov
Congressional Record, *February 5, 1980*

Prudence and Principles

I think it would be a great mistake to move too rapidly in this area. We have heard the legal outline from our able colleague, the gentlewoman from Illinois (Mrs. Collins), and some very practical suggestions from our colleague from Alabama. But I wonder if it would not be helpful if we looked at how we got involved in sanctions in the first place. This was not a judgment on any particular government. This was an action under international law, a request on the part of Great Britain, the colonial power which reported an illegal act on the part of Mr. Ian Smith and those with him in Rhodesia. We acquiesced and voted with Great Britain in the United Nations Security Council to impose the sanctions.

In doing that we put ourselves clearly on the side of law and order in the international field. That is where we ought to stay. We ought to consider, of course, the suffering of the people of that country and we should consider their human rights, which all of us have worked for, I am sure, for many years.

But as has been said here by our able colleague, the gentleman from Illinois (Mr. Erlenborn), and others, the interests of the United States should be the first concern of every member of this House. What is going to be the effect on our country? We need not serve as moral judges here, nor conduct a painstaking, nitpicking inspection of what this government may or may not be doing. I think the members of this House know I am not enraptured by the Popular Front. I have spoken about that before.

We cannot consider ourselves acting with prudent concern

for this country, if we move hastily to lift the sanctions. I think
the resolution expresses that prudence. I support it.

Debate on lifting sanctions against Rhodesia
Congressional Record, *June 28, 1979*

Mr. Chairman, I would like to speak to something else. I am
not going to make a fuss over this amendment. I approve of
our chairman's amendment. But, I just want to say this: I am
not in favor of giving U.S. money, or any money, to corrupt
and cruel governments, but I would hate to turn our backs on
the people of any country. To say that in times of starvation
in any country in the world, we are unwilling to give food to
the volunteer agencies, such as Catholic Relief, Lutheran Relief, or World Vision, the very good private organizations that
would deliver that food to the starving, is a scar on the hu-
manitarian tradition of this country.

I can remember as a very small child, food and aid going
out to China from the church in Bernardsville, because there
was a flood in the Yellow River basin. Nobody cared who
was sitting in the palace. The point was who was starving in
the streets. Under certain conditions, I would not give money
to the government. There, I agree with those who oppose aid.
But when we can be sure that a corrupt government would
not receive anything, I certainly would not want to close the
door on the possibility of charitable and humane contributions to starving people, no matter where they are.

*Debate on amendment prohibiting aid to the Socialist Republics of Vietnam,
Cambodia, and Cuba*
Congressional Record, *April 10, 1979*

Aid to the Third World

We must, we simply must, consider more carefully the people of the so-called "Third World." We must have some humility and recognize that they can teach us a lot about their countries, what's going to work there and what won't work, and where the pitfalls are. Because there are different kinds of pitfalls. We may think automatically that the pitfalls will be race, but with some countries it's tribes. It's very significant, I think, that Kenya, which began its independence with many important white government officials, soon filled those positions with black deputies, assistants, and so on. Now, there's only one white left in any position of importance. He's called McDonald and he's a Scot. He's the head of elections.

Now, why? Because there are several different tribes in Kenya. With a Scot who's been there for many years, there is no question of tribal influence in elections. If you're going to have free elections in a country where it is tribal differences, not racial differences, that are important, you'd better know.

This is something that is almost an obsession of mine. It's certainly my leading, guiding principle in foreign affairs. We must not act just because for us a program seems right and just, or even loving and idealistic. We should act because it's also a practical program, suited to the particular place and people because it's the only thing that's going to work. If we continue our present method of, as the French say, "de haut en bas" (from top bottom) of letting the flood of aid flow without any cooperation, initiative, or participation of the people who are at the receiving end, it's madness.

Have I mentioned Dr. Garret Harden, who wrote *The Limits of Altruism*—a very, very interesting and seminal book? He warns that it is not wise to pour food—and only food—into a country such as Bangladesh every single time they have a famine. Yes, people cannot starve, that is true, but there should be some arrangements with the local people to see what we can do about family planning clinics, food storage, and cooking fuels. With the increase in population, they keep cutting down the forest on the lower slopes of the Himalayas because they have to have fuel. And since we can't get family planning clinics going quickly enough, what we ought to do is to send with the food some kerosene for them to cook with. They've got to cook their food. They can't eat entirely raw food. And yet, the floods which cause the famines grow worse than ever because of the erosion on the hillsides.

One of the hopeful things that we ought to be talking about and offering them, the people in these countries that need fuel, are the new energy orchards that Secretary of Agriculture Berglund has told us about. The botanists are working, and this is particularly true of our big paper companies—Georgia Pacific, I think he mentioned, was one of them—and Weyerhaeuser. There's going to be a whole new species of trees which will be grown specifically because the leaves and twigs absorb more of the power of the sun. They will grow quickly and make a wonderful source of biomass electricity, maybe even gasohol fuel.

Perhaps that's something that we ought to be offering Bangladesh. Or, here's an idea from Woods Hole: Do you need protein, are you a nation with a seacoast or a big lake, like Bolivia or Chad? Well, here's a raft with long poles dangling from it: Put two little mussels on each of those poles. Then in due time all you have to do is row out and lift up the poles and you'll find they're covered with mussels. You don't have to feed mussels. There's no energy involved in doing it. You don't have to have a motor to get out there: You can row. And this produces protein.

The only person who ever seemed the slightest interested

in this was the previous ambassador from India. India could do this, of course, all along her coast.

The question is, are they interested. There's no use in forcing anything.

If Indians don't eat mussels or won't eat mussels—and people have extraordinary prejudices about food—maybe we need a process that would mash up the mussels and make them palatable in some other way. Bread, or mush, or something.

We must operate with humble understanding of local people and places. Nehru is quoted as giving a formula for progress in Asia, where 90 percent of the people are in agriculture: "Progress in Asia is giving a man who has a wooden plow the opportunity to get himself a metal plow." A metal plow, not a tractor he doesn't know how to repair, which needs gasoline and tires he cannot afford to buy. Too often we have, in all good will and benevolence, applied our ways and our systems to foreign ways.

One thing is clear: We can't continue our arrogant ways. It is true that very often we're pushed around, but the arrogance comes in the whole basic concept, that somehow we know best, that we have systems that are best. What we've done with agriculture is a miracle, but it is a miracle based on cheap gasoline and marvelously fertile, enormously wide lands. And these conditions are not true everywhere.

So there's no use our thinking that we have a system that's going to be universally applicable because it works here. We must be more intelligent, more thoughtful. We're going to have to have a whole different attitude.

Taped interview, November 12, 1980

I would like to say a word about the whole question of foreign aid. Yes, I think it is unpopular, and the reason why it is, is that the words, "foreign aid," have been bandied about irresponsibly as though some enormous sums were being poured out that would compare with the expense of the Defense Department or social security or welfare.

But let us ask the people of our districts, as I do of mine, "Do you want some food to go to this place? Do you want some medicine to go to cure river blindness in Africa?"

The answer is inevitably, "yes." The American people are not devoid of compassion or a sense of responsibility. Certainly our contribution to the international funds is the biggest, and so it should be.

Debate on foreign aid appropriations
Congressional Record, *July 18, 1979*

Mr. Chairman, I must rise in opposition to this amendment [to suspend foreign aid to OPEC countries including Nigeria]. We are talking now about one of the greatest nations of Africa. Its population has grown to 80 million people, and they cannot feed their people. They are using the money to buy food, but what they really need most urgently is this small seed money that can be directed by technological experts into the development of increased food production.

We cannot go on forever feeding the whole world. At the moment we have a surplus, and indeed Nigeria can and does buy some of it. But what we must do in these countries is to develop their production through technical assistance.

Debate on amendment to suspend foreign aid to OPEC nations,
including Nigeria
Congressional Record, *April, 4, 1979*

Respect for Others

Respect for others is a key in life. For instance, I always thought that one of the best examples of this was Eleanor Roosevelt when she went to India, and was photographed with her shoes off and garlanded and in rather ungainly position in some Indian ceremony. Another example was Pat Nixon, dressed up in a West African costume, trying to join in a dance with the West African ladies.

Now, both of them looked rather foolish, let's be honest, but that's the point of manners. You don't put your vanity above what is going to make other people happy and comfortable. And the ability to throw away such formal considerations, in the clear and obvious interest of somebody else's feelings, is a very important part of manners. You simply do not insist on your own way.

Another example was given me by a great friend of mine, Iris Origo, who is Anglo–American by birth. She was staying with me in the country, and a wonderful man, a Pennsylvania farmer by birth, was going to drive us to the airport. He came with his wife, because he didn't want to leave her to spend a lonely day. He thought she'd enjoy the ride, and he said to Iris, "Well, hi folks, how are you?"

And Iris, who is accustomed to saying, "How do you do?" said, "Hello, hello, hello," in her very English accent. Perfect response. I mean, that's the point. You don't make him uncomfortable by answering a well-meant, well-intentioned salutation with some stiff, correct formality.

Taped interview, April 25, 1980

The New Decade

This is the time of prophecy and remembrance—the end of a year, the beginning of a new decade. Pundits prophesy as to what we may expect in the 80s; others recapitulate the fads and fashions and events of the decade just ended.

This report will be concerned with a few thoughts which, one hopes, were and will be part of our continuing values. The first is an excerpt from William Faulkner's address when he received the Nobel Prize for literature in 1950:

> Our tragedy today is a general and universal physical fear so long sustained by now that we can even bear it. There are no longer problems of the spirit. There is only the question: When will I be blown up? Because of this, the young man or woman writing today has forgotten the problems of the human heart in conflict with itself . . .
>
> He must learn them again, he must teach himself that the basest of all things is to be afraid, and teaching himself that, forget it forever, leaving no room . . . for anything but the old verities and truths of the heart, the old universal truths lacking which any story is ephemeral and doomed—love and honor and pity and pride and compassion and sacrifice. Until he does so, he labors under a curse. He writes not of love but of lust, of defeats in which nobody loses anything of value, of victories without hope and, worst of all, without pity or compassion. His griefs grieve on no universal bones, leaving no scars. He writes not of the heart but of the gland.
>
> Until he relearns these things, he will write as though he stood among and watched the end of man. I do not believe in the end of man. It is easy enough to say that man is immortal simply because he will endure: that when the last ding-dong of doom has clanged and faded from the last worthless rock hanging tideless

in the last red and dying evening, that even then there will still be one more sound: that of his puny inexhaustible voice still talking. I believe more than this. I believe man will not merely endure, he will prevail. He is immortal, not because he, alone among creatures, has an inexhaustible voice, but because he has a soul, a spirit, capable of compassion and sacrifice and endurance . . . courage and honor and hope and pride and compassion and pity . . . which have been the glory of his past.

The second comes from Eric Hoffer, philosopher and former longshoreman:

> . . . it may well be that the survival of the species will depend upon the capacity to foster a boundless capacity for compassion. In the alchemy of man's soul, almost all noble attributes—courage, love, hope, faith, beauty, loyalty—can be transmuted into ruthlessness. Compassion alone stands apart from the continuous traffic between good and evil proceeding within us.

A third voice is T. S. Eliot's, in "Choruses" from *The Rock:*

> The world turns and the world changes;
> But one thing does not change.
> In all of my years, one thing does not change.
> However you disguise it, this thing does not change:
> The perpetual struggle of Good and Evil.

An echo of this is in what Dr. Kenneth B. Clark wrote in *The Pathos of Power:* "The most serious threat to the survival of mankind is not now ignorance in the traditional sense, but a morally neutral, that is, an inhibited human intelligence."

And, finally, when Mahatma Gandhi was asked, "What do you most fear?" He answered, "The hardness of heart of the educated."

Fortunately, there are many signs that compassion has not failed, that education does not always harden the heart. According to the research service of the Library of Congress, tax returns filed in 1978 showed $29.5 billion given by individuals to charities here at home; consider also these small, spontaneous expressions of the same emotion extended to faraway strangers in Cambodia and to our fellow citizens imprisoned in Iran: The children of St. Joseph's School for the Deaf in St. Louis, Missouri, who collected $23.16 for aid to

Cambodia; the thousand students in West Windsor High School who organized a meeting and signed a proclamation of concern for the hostages held in our embassy in Teheran; the ecumenical meeting in the Anshe Emeth synagogue in New Brunswick, where Catholics, Jews and Protestants—blacks and whites—gathered over $10,000 for Cambodia in one morning.

The imagination and sensitivity that are among the sources of compassion have been evident in thousands of such meetings all over the United States. Every congressman and senator could recite similar outpourings of kindly feeling—of the "compassion and pity and sacrifice" which, as Faulkner said, have been part of the glory of man's past. That they are still very much a part of our tradition and our daily lives is something for which we can all be grateful as we end this year and start the new decade.

Newsletter, *January 16, 1980*